HISTORY OF CANVEY ISLAND

5 GENERATIONS

by Susan White.

Published by
The Bookshop,
27 b High Street,
Canvey Island,
Essex

First published in Great Britain
1994 by the Bookshop, High Street,
Canvey Island, Essex.

Second reprint 1998

ISBN 978-178035-098-1

Bibliography

Three years volumes of "The Essex Countryside".
The History of South East Railways.
Port of London Authorities Literature.
How the Lands faired. (D. Nicholls).

CONTENTS

I DEDICATE THIS BOOK TO MY GREAT GRANDFATHER WILLIAM JOHN ROBERT FENWICK BORN 1ST OCT. 1874.
AND MY GREAT NEPHEW JOE BRADLEY WHITE BORN 14TH JUNE 1994.

Introduction

I started this book as a thesis on Canvey Island whilst at Teacher's Training College in the Lake District in 1968, that is where the research finished. I have done my best to update the last 25 years.

Much of this evidence is from first hand sources as there is very little material for research and it seems as thought the historical writers have considered this area as rather a backwater, as far as society is concerned. (But all least I can state as a fact that any islander will open an eye when the local pub is mentioned to a visitor, for Charles Dickens knew about us. In his novel, 'Great Expectations', he refers to the Lobster Smack and to its four poster beds).

Part I research is from first hand information from Dr. E. Linden, who lived in one of the orginal Dutch cottages of which only three remain today. These are illustrated in part 2.

Although Canvey Island was first settled by a few dutch immigrants in 1621 the main emphasis of development is from the early 1900's whereby the first stafe to link the island to the mainland gave access to the influx of the main core of settlers.

From here initiates the growth of Canvey Island as an important urban centre and holiday resort and plays a predominantly important role whereby the organisation has had meet the heavy demands of the London overspill especially since the post-was period.

I would like to thank many local inhabitants for their recorded memories and especially Mr. A. Alamba local councillors, Mr. A. Mason, Mr. H. George and Dr. Linton for their information.

I would also like to mention my Grand-father the late Mr. John Fenwick who supplied me with some of the photoprints from which his Model Village of Canvey Island was based. The Village was situated at the corner of Furtherwick Road where now stands the car Accessories Shop and later on Canvey sea front, unfortunately when my Grand-father died my brother Brian White intended to keep the village going, but it was destroyed by vandals the first day he opened it for the season, but my Grand-father work still remains to this day, there is a model made by him of the old Dutch Cottage in the Museum at Northwick corner.

It was in the early part of the century that my Great Grand-father Mr. William Fenwick came down to Canvey on Mr. Hester's special train with a view to buying a plot of ground to build a holiday bungalow to where he could bring his wife and family for weekends and holidays from London to Canvey's fresh air, he did buy a plot in Wagenham Drive, which has now been named Chapman Road, as it was the road opposite to where the old Chapman Lighthouse was situated.

It was coincidental that my Great-Grand-father came originally to buy land at Sixty Acres, and it is my brother Brian White that is the instigator of the development now taking place.

The house that my Great Grand-father built with the help of my Grand-father still stands today. My Grand-father built many holiday bungalows at Leigh Beck, and was one of the first builders to have building materials from Canvey Supply Company, a lot of these holiday bungalows are still standing but with modifications. My father George White has built in the region of 140 houses, and my brother considerably more, and now my two nephews Paul and Scot White are also in the building trade Paul having built his own house at Sixty Acres, making five generation of builders on Canvey Island.

Canvey Island lies on the north side of the Thames Estuary about thirty miles east of London. The Island is four miles long and two miles wide at its greatest width, the circumference is about thirteen miles, its four thousand acres of flat marshland are entirely enclosed by a high seawall which alone prevents the Island from being flooded at every spring tide, almost the whole of the island lies below high water mark.

The River Thames has played a dominant role in the history of Canvey Island since man first settled there. The difference in level between the land and the river has never been more than a few feet, therefore any change in a relative level, however small, has had a significant effect upon the coastline. Although these changes have been taking place throughout history, it is onlly in comparatively recent years that geologists have begun to study the minor movements of the land surface which are still taking place today.

Sources of Anglo Dutch Conflict

The Dutch community had not been on Canvey may years, before it found itself with several difficult problems regarding their English neighbours. The first, and perhaps the most serious was the religious conflict. The Dutch who were Presbyterians had erected their own Chapel after obtaining permission from King Charles, the services were conducted in the Dutch language, this soon became a source of ill feeling between the two nationalities on the Island. The English residents had no option but to make the long journey across the Island onto the mainland, travelling across the Hadleigh Ray to attend the Church of St. Mary or "Benfleet come Canvey" as it came to be called. Eventually matters came to a head when one of the English families refused to pay tithes to the parish priest, on the grounds that they received none of the spiritual benefits to which they were entitled. The priest suggested that the English people on the Island should provide a place of worship, but when they appealed to the Dutch for permission to use their Chapel for services occasionally, they were refused. The Dutch were most probably afraid, that if they permitted the English to use their Chapel, they might forfeit the privilege of holding services in their native tongue. There was heated exchange of views, if not blows outside the Dutch Chapel on Whit Monday 1956, the English were defeated. The Dutch Chapel continued to be used by the Dutch community until 1704.

The perennial problem of the marshland water, was another source of friction, before the dutch wall was built wildfowl provided a useful subsidiary source of income to the marshmen, but when the dutch settled there, they began to cultivate the soil. There is plenty of corroborative evidence that they were engaged largely in cultivation. In 1638 for instance, the Minister Cornelius Jacobson was summoned to London to explain as to why he had made so little return from the farming of land which had been represented to the Dutch Church on by Heinrich Brouwer, he complained that with the exception of one good barley harvest, the land had yielded poor crops, apparently the harvests improved, for in the following year he was able to pay arrears of rent £6.2.6. to another Dutchman, Nicholas Pelseeve, whose tenant he was.

It is understood he did not come to England to undertake this relatively minor work of reclamation, his main object was to drain the ground level, and he only accepted this commission as a stop-gap pending completion of the negotiations for the major task in the fens. Heinrick Brouwer shares in Canvey Amsterdam in 1637 says that Vermuyden obtained shares in Canvey Island through his acquaintance with Joan Goppenburg whilst in London 1622, the Dutch engineers built the wall from the marsh clay available on the spot as was the usual practise in land reclamation they faced the main wall along the river Thames with stone, brought to the site from elsewhere probably Kent, this would have been quite easy by barge. The broad ditch which runs parallel to the sea-wall plays an important part in the drainage system, the smaller inlets in the marshes were filled in, so the drainage was concentrated into the main ditch which was allowed to discharge into the river through seven main sluices. These later became known as Commissioners Dykes and did not belong to the owners of the property through which they ran. Although the agreement was originally signed by Joan Croppenburg alone, it is clear that Vermuyden obtained the necessary capital by borrowing on the security of the one third of the land enclosed. The capital probably came from Holland.

When the wall was completed a considerable number of Dutch workmen settled on the Island as farmers. In 1628 Cornelius Vermuyden received a knighthood, also in this year the hundred or so "Low County Stranger's" employed on Canvey "filling and husbanding of ground" petitioned King Charles for permission to hold services in the Dutch language.

On 21st December 1631 the Dutch community elected Cornelius Jacobson as the Minister, agreeing to pay him three pence for every acre in their possession, on condition that, as long as the land does not produce anything.

So was established the Dutch community on Canvey Island, a curious enclosure of foreigners on a little Island, a closely knit community.

Is it quite likely that in this submergence Canvey Island became an island for the first time, and aquired a shape, similar to which it is today. The settlements were wiped out, and instead of a thriving community Canvey became desolate and uninhabitable, a dense expanse of marsh saltings. This was the place which the Anglo Saxon named Canvey or "The Island of Canas People".

The Community of Shepherds.

The centuries between the mid Roman period and the Norman Conquest were a period of intensive settlement and agricultural development throughout England, and by the end of that period the main rural framework of England as we know it today had been established. All along the thames Estuary Anglo-Saxon settlement in South Essex. There can be no doubt that the marshland pastures of Canvey Island were bought in service by these early settlers for grazing sheep.

The Island was low lying and probably subject to periodic flooding which rendered it unsuitable for permanent settlement. Canvey was habited by large flocks of sheep, a tiny community of shepherds living in crude temporary shelters guarded their flocks from the dangers of spring tides, which when came flooded up the many creeks and inlets.

The Netherlandish Community.
The Building of the Dutch Sea-wall.

In September 1621 the sea wall at Dagenham in Essex, which had already been repaired in 1593 was again breached, and the young Dutch engineer Corneluis Vermuyden was commissioner to superivise the work of enclosure. This is the first mention of Vermuyden in connection with the Thames Estuary, and indeed the first record of his arrival in England.

Canvey Island in Roman Times

The existence of Roman British settlement on Canvey Island has been established on sound evidence believing that their main purpose was the making of salt by the evaporation of sea water. The existence of Red Hills all along the Essex coast suggests that there were many other salt making communities at this time. The Canvey salt works located as they were on the busy Thames Estuary, may well have been of considerable importance in the early Roman period, and this may explain the discovery of a Roman road leading from a point on the mainland opposite the most northerly point of Canvey Island, to a large Roman encampment at Chelmsford. No trace of this road exists on the Island itself, but there would have been no need to embark in those days. Some Historians including Camden, have argued that Canvey is in fact the island called Counes which Ptolemy shows on his map of arca circa A.D. 100. They appear to base their argument in the similarity of name. This hardly seems tenable, however the name is of Anglo-Saxon origin and the geological evidence suggests that Canvey may well have been part of the mainland in the first century. This seems evidence gives a possible clue to the where abouts of Counas: The land is placed by Ptolemy in the outer estuary, and in view of the land submergence in mid-Roman times it is quite likely that before this took place there was an Island there, which was never re-appeared, comparable perhaps to the Goodwin Sands. Such an Island would have course been very familiar to the navigators from whom Ptolemy gathered his information, for it lay across the entrance to a much frequented channel. On these grounds we must reject the attractive notion that Canvey Island appeared on one of the earliest maps ever made. Never the less it convenient to pass through the district on the way to their encampments inland.

Some time toward the end of the second century a great submergence must have overwhelmed the community of salt makers on Canvey, and indeed all the similar communities on both banks of the estuary. The evidence suggests that this was no gradual sinking of the land, to that which is now taking place, but a sudden catastrophe.

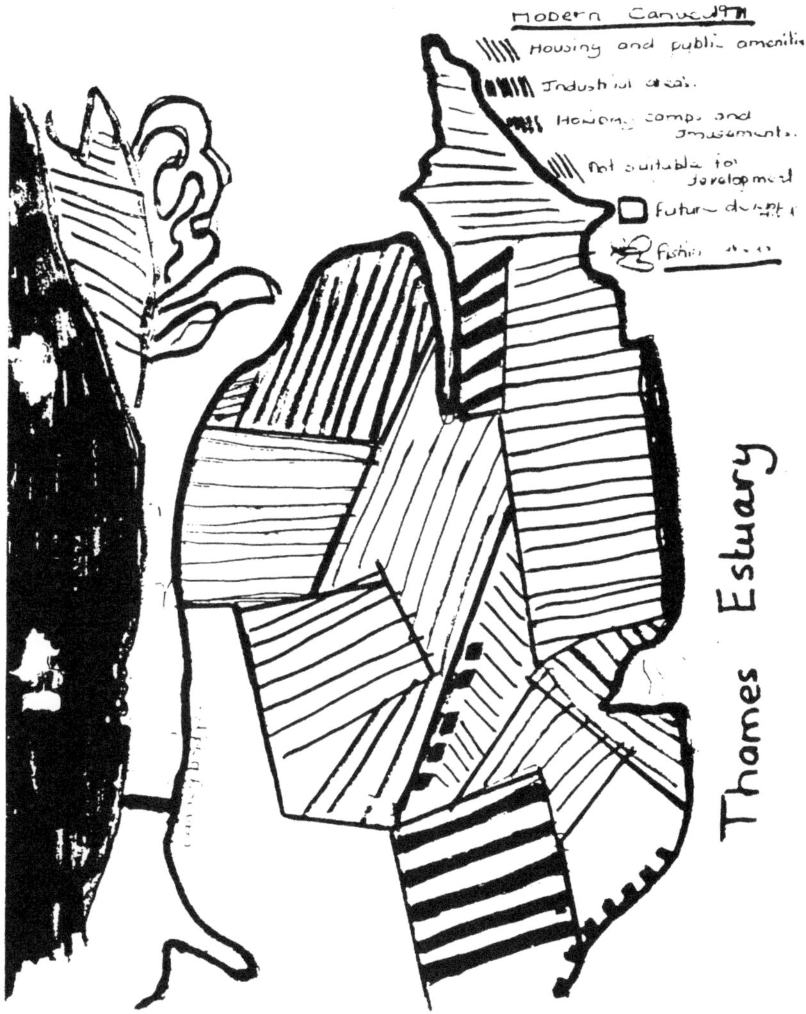

Modern Canvey
Housing and public amenities
Industrial areas.
Holiday camps and amusements.
Not suitable for development
Thames Estuary

These movements, though very gradual are cumulative, and in the long run are of great importance. Geological evidence supplemented by the results of systematic level taking, suggests that the South East of England is subsiding at the rate of about eight inches every hundred years. This filting has been going on for at least three hundren years at about the same rate, and some geologists have suggested that it has in fact been going on since the late Glacial period.

The geological evidence of a land subsistence is strongly supported by archeological discovery, not only in the Thames Estuary but elsewhere on the coasts of England and Wales, remains have been discovered in localitites which suggest that where they were originally deposited the land surface must have been considerably higher above sea level than it is today.

On Canvey Island and elsewhere on the Essex coast the archeological evidence is based on what are called the Red Hills. There are several of these low moulds in a line along the Southern shore of the Island, and they have yielded important archeological remains. The moulds obtain their name from the fact that they are composed of burnt earth are fire earths of various depths and the remains of pottery of the first and second centuries A.D. which appear to be fragments of the large earthernware pans manufactured on the site and used for the evaporation of salt. The Red Hills now lie below the level of the spring tides, but it is obvious that when they were first settled they must have been at least four or five feet above the high water mark, if so the land surface of Canvey Island must have subsided by about fifteen feet since Roman times. This conclusion fitted the known rate of subsistence in recent timed, that Mr. E. Linden in a paper to the Geologists Association in 1940 postulated that the present rate of subsistence had in fact continued ever since the first century.

Sluice farm, which was formerly situated at the Northwick side of The Lobster Smack, now demolished

The Maintenance of Worship

For almost two hundred years, though the outward appearance of the Island may have changed a little, its community life was almost the same. English families came to farm the lands vacated by the Dutch, although in many cases the Landlords were still Dutch and they appeared to follow very much the same pattern of farming as their predecessors. The only events which occurred to enliven the community were connected with the church, of the old public house, down by Hole haven Creek, which still stands and is used just as much today, attracting many visitors to the Island. Apart from their agricultural duties the main energies of the community were absorbed in three directions, and maintenance of worship, the roadways and the walls.

The first real break with the past was the arrival on the scene of a Church of England curate in 1709 and the pulling down of the old Dutch chapel, which was replaced by a church capable of accommodating eighty people, dedicated to St. Catherine. The new structure was concentrated by the Bishop of London on the 11th June 1712. This church still stands today, but has not been in use for the last 5 or 6 years, a new modern church has been built about half a mile away. There were no wealthy families actually living on the Island in these times, and the building of the church was made possible by one of the absent landlords of Canvey, a Mr Edgar of the Victualling Office. There is no trace of this name in the earlier records of landownership on the Island, and the interesting theory has been arrived at, that in fact this was none other than Mr. Otger the Dutch patron of the original Dutch Chapel who had angliased his name. There is some evidence that other Dutch residents on Canvey had angliased their names, for instance the John Bell who was living on the Island in 1742 between Thomas Hanson and the daughter of a Dutch family on the Island. The new church was poorly endowed. The sum of ten pound had been allotted to enable a curate to visit the Island to preach a course of twenty sermons a year "wind and weather permitting" The Community could not support a resident Minister, because the titles went to the incumbents of the nine parishes, between which the Island was divided.

The Rector of Stifford which lies on the mainland, made a reference to this in his first sermon in the new Church on Canvey "It is a pity the endowment is now larger, that there might have been sufficient maintenance for the Minister but what is wanting is an effectual provision of lands and tithes, for this sacred use and purpose, it is to be hoped, that it will be sufficiently made up by the generosity and voluntary contributions of my brethren, to whom the care of the souls of this Island is committed".

This hope was largely unfulfilled, although the incumbent of the nine parishes, did later contribute a total sum of £17. per annum towards the expense of the Church.

Since there was no resident Minister, the Church was closed down during the week, although of course it may have not been altogether deserted, for the smugglers certainly had caches there for their contraband, it was opened only at weekends during the summer months, when the curate came across from South Benfleet to deliver the stipulated twenty sermons per annum. On these occasions a flag was flown from the Church Steeple to warn the parishioners, and also no doubt the smugglers, that a service was to be held. Even during the summer months the journey across the creek was not easy, and in the winter it was regarded as unpractical. The Church was closed down altogether during the winter.

St. Catherine's Church erected in 1712 had not been built very substantial and was practically rebuilt in 1745, this time rededicated to St. Peter. The church timber construction, which was all the poor community on the Island could afford, did not stand up well to the climate. The present Church on the site although built of timber was given a coating of cement, the rebuilding in 1745 was erected partly by public subscription, but mainly through a benefactor named Scratton, a landowner on the Island, who lived at Prittlewell, and gave part of the Vicar of Prittlewell, to enable him to perform divine service in the new Church. He gave a further £10 to the Minister duly appointed to preach the course of twenty sermons per annum.

584.
WATERSIDE F

Agriculture Depression

Cheap wheat began to flood into England from the New World in the early 1870, and soon swept away the traditional basis of agriculture in South Essex. The heavy sticky clays were difficult soils to plough, three horse land, it was called, and although they gave good yields, the costs of cultivation were high. However the Essex farmers had become so accustomed to corn growing, that they could not readily adjust themselves to the changed conditions, by turning to the production of milk or livestock. In the first years following 1875 the clay-land farmers suffered another severe setback from a series of bad harvests, which co-incide with the low prices of wheat, and caused such distress in agricultural areas, that in 1880 the Government set up the Richmond Commission to investigate the position. A Mr. Drue in his report to the Commission had a depressing account to give of the conditions in South Essex. "There are a very large number of farms in the Landlord's hands, some of which are practically, although not actually, uncultivated. As also seen in several parts of the Country, the state of agriculture was deplorable. Some land was altogether derelict, and more were full of weeds and natural grasses which a few cattle were picking up a bare living, farm houses were empty, or only occupied by over-lookers or caretakers, in some cases a lot of cottages were also empty. The general appearance of the county was desolate". Fourteen years later the Royal Commission on Agriculture Distress, submitted another report to the government, which was even more alarming.

The land speculators followed in the wake of the bankrupt farmers, and bought up the land for little more than a song. In fact all over South Essex there sprang up a host of temporary and often ramshackle dwellings, erected by the new owners on small plots of land, and in Canvey Island the same process was taking place. The Lands facing the river, were naturally the first to be acquired. Some thousand acres were bought by a gentleman named Mr. Hester, who proceeded to divide them into small plots, for sale on a system of easy payment, thus enabling many people to become a freehold of land, in the easiest possible manner.

Here was yet another constant source of irritation, for as the memory of the original enclosure faded, and a new generation of Dutch people were born, not only among the settlers on the Island but among the distant Dutch landowners, so the responsibility for wall repairs must have seemed increasingly onerous among the settlers on the Island, and they resented having to maintain the wall, when there English neighbours with twice as much land benefited twice as much, and paid not a penny towards the cost. The gradual land subsistence was continuing all the time, thus the erosions of the banks gave constant trouble. Just how the Dutchmen arranged for the repairs of the sea-wall is unknown, but their lands became known as "Third Acre Lands" and the owners were called upon to pay a special "Third Acre" tax, towards the upkeep of the walls. It was because of that, the conveyance of "Third Acre Lands" in 1623 specified that the acreage of the lands should be conveyed down to the nearest road, instead of in very vague terms as was usual with marshland conveyancing.

One final source of conflict may be mentioned although its importance should not be exagerrated. When the Dutch refugees from Catholic persecution began to arrive in England in the sixteenth century, they were received with a sympathetic welcome, many of them settled in Colchester, and established the busy industry there. Early in the seventeenth Century however, the political climate changed drastically, hardly had the Dutch settled on Canvey, when the massacre of Amboyna took place (1623) and events which greatly incensed the English, and caused a long period of commercial rivalry and wars. The middle years of the century were largely occupied with this conflict, it reached a climax in 1667 when the Dutch Admiral De. Ruyter sailed up the Thames Estuary, and burnt our finest ships as they anchored in the River Medway, Kent Parliament having paid off the crews in anticipation of an early peace. Canvey figured prominently in these events, for the Dutch sailors landed on the Island presumably, in search of provisions and caused considerable damage to property. Sir Henry Appleton wrote to the Secretary of State after the incident "The Dutch have landed on Canvey and have damaged, barns and eight houses, and taken several small boats".

Canvey Island was one of the earliest coastal marshes to come under the plough. As late as 1795 an agricultural writer said "of the marshes, the sea coasts, and the lands which have been produced by, and embanked at different periods from the sea, were them had been brought under the plough". This may be compared with the observation of Daniel Defoe in 1722. Is that an observable portion of them have been brought under the plough". along the North shore of the River Thames, which are held by farmers, cow keepers and grazing butchers who live in and near London, and that they are generally stocked with large fat sheep" Thus, at a time when the traditional economy of the coastal marshes took to pasturing sheep and cattle, the little Dutch community of Cavey Island was turning to cultivation. Friction was inevitable because the water requirements were different from those of pastures. The English residents, most of whom were engaged upon livestock farming, wanted the water level in the drainage ditches to be kept sufficiently high to ensure adequate water for their stock, whereas the Dutch were more anxious to keep their fields adequately drained. More ever the English probably resented the fact of the enclosure, and subsequent drainage upon the traditional marshland harvest of eels and wildfowl. They did not go to the lengths of compatriots in the fens in taking up arms against the reclaims, but they gave vent to their feelings in the words of this ballad.

Our smaller rivers are now dry land,
The eels are turned to serpents there,
And if old Father Thames play not the man,
Then farewell to all good English men,
Why should we stay then and perish with thirst,
To the new world in the moon, they away let us go,
For if the Dutch Colony get there first,
Tis a thousand to one, they'll drain that too,

In the original agreement the Dutch had undertaken not only to reclaim the land, but also to maintain the walls at their own expense.

The plots were so conveniently small, that each person can possess himself or herself according to their means, of a sufficent quantity of land to errect a bungalow, villa or shop.

Leigh Beck farm, about 1905. Once the residence of Canvey's first developer, Mr Frederick Hester. (Now demolished).

Farming Days on Canvey before it was built up, was described as a 'great green walled park'. Very little remains today but the names Furtherwick, Southwick etc., Canvey had considerable number of farms, most have gone, or are used for other purposes, like Waterside which is now a thriving Sports Centre and swimming pool, this was near the Canvey-Benfleet Bridge. According to local history Scar House Farm was possibly the oldest Canvey Farm, it was given its description to a part of the southern Island seawall, Scars Elbow.

Thought to Belloven's Farm

Scar House farm.

Some say it came from the black rocks on the sea wall Hill Hall Farm was in the old days on the Canvey Road, there was a farm off of Further wick Road near Chambers Dairies, a Northwick Farm which I can remember, when I was a child I lived for a while on Northwick Camp whilst waiting for a council house, I can remember various barns dotted about in the area, some of these were used and some empty, the empty ones making very good play areas. Farmer Layzell lived in the Farmhouse half way down Northwick, we used to pick his youngest daughter Dawn up in the taxi that took all children from Northwick to school.

My parents can remember Farmer Claydon from Leigh Beck Farm, Farmer Cook from the Winter Gardens area, Farmer and Councillor Leach from Waterside Farm, Farmer Cass from the vicinity of Canvey Village, Norris's Farm which is still around today. My father often used to take Farmer White in his taxi, his farm was Sluice Farm on the Northwick side of The Lobster Smack, now demolished.

Before the bridge was built one could often see cattle being driven from Canvey to Benfleet at low tide, also barges could be seen, complete with haystack, they were known as "stackies", and often a boy sat on the top as a navigator, the lush green grass was being taken from Canvey to London and later fed to Derby winners.

Knightswick Farm was just off Somnes Avenue, it was part of the original development of the Winter Gardens area. Small Gains Farm was on the left hand side of the corner of Small Gains Corner which was used for boat building after the second World War Mr. Sullivan a popular rag and bone man who when any charity held Jumble Sales would buy anything left over which would boost the funds, he had his sorting out establishment in this old Barn. It has now been demolished. Southwick Farm, which was also known as White's Farm was opposite Hawksbury Road. The Island Farm was just over the seawall opposite The Island Yacht Clubs landing jetty, it was surrounded by a large lake. Now redeveloped.

Typical of the area at that time. This shows a cart shed - and sheep.

This century Canvey Island has grown as an urban centre and has roles to play as a holiday, residential and industrial community.

Easily reached from London and Southend by road and by electric trains via Benfleet station, modern Canvey is well known to thousands of people who come to enjoy the long sandy beaches and the excellent bathing.

Residentially, Canvey grows in popularity each decade as more and more London based commuters realise that, within easy reach of their work is a pleasant place to live within sight and sound of the sea and with plenty of elbow room to live in spacious style.

As Canvey grew in importance, industrially, the agricultural aspect has steadily declined to give way to a more balanced and prospering economy, thus the large farms of grazing land were carefully divided to make way for urban development.

At the turn of the century began the development that was to turn Canvey into a residential town and resort. The chief instigator was called Mr. Hester who was conscious of "London's teeming and tailing millions" who had been awakened by the possibility of a "holiday at sea". he envisaged supplying mirky London with yet another lung. He proposed transforming Canvey Island into a premier Holiday resort. The completion of the main line railway between London and Shoeburyness virtually Victorian enterprising speculators on numerous new development in the South-East corner of the country.

Mr. Hester realised that the ultimate success of the scheme depended largely on a plan to provide the Thames side marshland with better internal communications and decided to build his own monorail tramway. At the time it proved to be quite a revolutionary concept in any public transport undertaking. As the second edition of Daly's History of Canvey Island, published in 1902, proudly states "With regard to the mono metal tramway, it will always be renowned to the credit of Canvey Island that it inaugurated this novel and rapid system of locomotion in England.

The plan was to link the ferry landing stage at Benfleet Creek, which also served the main line station nearby to the new pier and esplanade, then under construction on the south side of the island facing the Thames. As an added attraction the monorail would run close to the exotic Winter Garden Palace, also under construction, which was designed to be one of the largest and most unusual of its kind in the south-east, or indeed anywhere.

The Monorail System

Work on the monorail system began in earnest during 1901-1902, and a single steel track, and a number of lay-by laps which allowed cars to pass each other en route, was laid over a distance covering about three miles. It run close to the old Dutch Counter sea wall through the Winter Gardens area to Lakeside, where it ran due west alongside the present High Street to Small Gains Corner. It continued along point Road to the spot where a sharp turn led to the terminus close to the projected pier.

After Mr. Hester became bankrupt, many of the people he had already sold land to, pitched tents, placed caravans and even old railway carriages on their plot of land, enabling them to spend weekends and holidays on the Island. One by one these temporary living quarters were replaced by wooden sheds, which were later extended to wooden holiday bungalows, some owners even living there permanently although they were scattered few and far between. Gradually after the war most of the existing places were occupied, but the area was without services, and a planning embargo was placed on Sixty Acres after the 1953 floods. When the sea defence programme and a drainage system costing £2.6 million was complete on Canvey, it made the site a possibility once more.

Castle Point District Council originally had given details to more than 80 national firms, of these only two had indicated interest but had not gone head.

During October 1986 Mrs. Margaret Willis, Chairman Castle Point Planning Committee, officially launched the prestigiuos Sixty Acres site by cutting the white ribbon at a champagne opening after years of struggling to get it off the ground. There were many difficulties that had, had to be tackled as the site was owned by many people, properties had to be brought and negotiations made between the existing owners and the developers, many opted for a new house in place of land, as a lot of these bungalows where on quite large plots. At this time they where living under terrible conditions with no proper toilets, water or gas supplies, after years of lorries and cars running on unmade roads, many of the roads where impassable especially in the winter. Mrs. Margaret Willis said it was a triumph for the Canvey firm B.G.White Ltd., that it was prepared to undertake the scheme which national firm's would not undertake, she also paid tribute to Don Reay Chief Planning Officer, Alan Finch Chief Technical Officer, Councillors Mrs. Joy Whiting and Mr. Bill Sharp, and their council officials.

Since the day when the official opening of Canvey bridge took place in 1931 countless cars, coaches and processions of vehicles of all kinds have crossed the narrow waters of Benfleet Creek.

For centuries this mirky channel had effectively separated Canvey from the mainland and it proved a serious obstacle to any plans for large scale development, With the disappointment of the monorail plus the fact of no way to cross the Island to the mainland, comparatively few people were attracted to settle. Regarded by most as a hindrance, this small creek however, had helped considerably to preserve the atmosphere of rural calm and openness which for so long had characterised these wide and wind swept marshes bordering the Thames.

Long before the arrival of the Norman Conquerors Essex men had known the value of these riverside marshes that provided such good grazing for their herds of cattle and the large flocks of sheep. The day was not far off when Britain's wealth was to become reckoned in wool, and wool from the Essex marshes at that. Farmers hereabouts certainly knew the real value of these pastures, and until the end of the nineteenth century Canvey was divided among a number of mainland parishes each of which jealousy guarded its important grazing rights on the island.

For generations men strove to make a safer crossing place on to the Island and year after year one reads of cartloads of gravel and larger stones being dumped on to the soft bed of the creek to create a firm crossing place at low tide. Eventually this object was achieved and "Benfleet hard" became the accepted crossing place for pedestrians and vehicles alike.

Several suggestions were made towards the turn of the century for the provision of a proper bridge on the island but nothing came of them. Such a small community hardly warranted a bridge so for many years the stepping stones and the hard remained the only ways of getting on or off the island at low tide. Once the tide had turned however, these routes were cut off and the only way across the creek then was by means of the small ferryboat that operated throughout the year.

At small gains a branch line was planned to serve the water side jetty which then existed in the creek to accommodate barges that brought large supplies of timber and ballast to the island, which of course initiated the price of land to 300 at the end of the 19th to 583 at the 1911 census.

The pioneer developer planned also to extend his railway over the waters of the creek so that it would connect with the mainland railway.

Passengers were to be accommodated in a grandiose tramcar which was designed to balance simply on two wheels, one at the front and one at the rear and which ran along the slender track supported by the weight and forward thrust of the thorough bred horse that was harnessed to a wooden frame so that it could help propel this unusual vehicle. Each tramcar was open-sided and built to carry sixteen passengers or thereabouts, who sat on upholstered benches under a canopy type roof. The driver-cum-conductor, dressed like some Ruritanian prince, sat on a small open platform from which he was to control the carriage and give a running commentary on the journey to the delighted passengers.

Alas! an untimely lack of funds prevented the completion of most or these enterprising plans and his schemes to electrify the tramway had to be abandoned.

However, the monorail ran for a short time and those who still recall paying a few coppers for a short ride on this novel conveyance "through fields of waving corn" and in 1902 Daly noted that "it is now possible to travel by mono-metal tramway, under cover through a delightful vista of floriculture.

Until 1926 Canvey Island, together with Benfleet, formed part of the Rochford Rural District an extensive area that stretched from the Thames to the Crouch. In 1926 Canvey Island was separated from this area and formed into an urban district.

The newly formed urban council set itself to develop the island as quickly as possible.

The year 1931 saw, with the opening of the bridge across to Benfleet, the removal of the last obstacle to real progress. This was of vital importance to Canvey progress for until this time traffic had either to ford the creek or cross by stepping stones.

The necessary capital of course was a difficult aspect. As early as 1825, advertisements were appearing in newspapers with the view of raising money off of the Norfolk, Suffolk and Essex Railroad Company which proposed a main line and several branch lines to cover the counties concerned. It was pointed out that the engineering difficulties in such flat countryside would be small. The sum required was £1,000,000 and the directors must have thought the money would pour in as only few days were given to prospective applicants in which to pay in their deposits. But the response seems to have been very disappointing,

The London and Essex Railway, which later changed to the Great Eastern Railway which was initiated in 1831. This brought a little more enthusiasm, but again in spite of glowing promises of quick returns, the prospectus failed. In 1834 another prospectus was put forward and had to be withdrawn but in 1836, through the energies of the directors, and further backing by some of the existing shareholders, the amount of capital required was almost raised.

After lengthy discussions with local land-owners the proprietors of the ferry and the various public bodies affected by the scheme it was finally agreed to commence work on the building of a bridge costing in the region of £15,000. The first pile was driven into the ooze of the river bed at a special ceremony performed by the Lord-Lieutenant of the country in 1930.

When the new bridge was officially opened my mother who was then 6 years old can remember the school children cubs and scouts lining up each side of the road, and the Girl's Life Brigade of which she was a cadet under the watchful eyes of Captain Margaret Kingley and Lts. Jessis Cass and Freda Hall forming a guard of honour. My mother has always said she is sure that these good ladies helped form the character of many Canvey girl, as in those days according to her the Girl's Life Brigade was one of the highlights of childhood on Canvey.

The new bridge was designed so that its 300-foot span would adequately carry a twenty foot carriage way and a single footpath across the creek. The entire structure supported on a number of wooden and metal piles, was engineered so that twin thirty centre section would retract on rollers over the fixed portion of the bridge. When opened this left a sixty foot gap through which all the largest pleasure craft using the creek could pass. Electrically operated this centre section could be opened of closed in a few minutes and in theory there was only brief traffic delay but if the nearby level crossing gates were closed to allow passing trains through a queue of traffic would sometimes stretch literally for miles at bank holiday weekends. For those trying to leave the Island after a pleasant time by the sea it was hardly the end of a perfect day.

British Rail

"Forgotten Railway Dreams" was the popular talk of this area and Essex might have had quite a dense network of railways if some of the dreams of the early railway promoters had been fulfilled. To build railways the need was more often people than money. Many booklets were produced by the Railway Companies to stimulate the traffic. A good example of its fanciful prose is "The fresh air of the Thames estuary circulates freely".

One of the last ferrymen was a Mr. Fred Edwards, who lived in South Benfleet and there was a small ferryman's cottage built on the side of the creek close to the spot where the present bridge stands. Crossing on the ferryboat was a matter of a couple of coppers, bicycles extra of course and in all weathers visitors and residents alike were rowed across the narrow waters, which have been known to freeze on more than one occasion within living memory.

With the opening of the Railway and the eastward expansion of London and its suburbs and islands population increased steadily over the years, and in the 1920's it was realised that something more permanent was needed for the convenience people living on the island or visiting it. More and more people were choosing the peace and quiet of an inexpensive home by the sea, and in the late 1920's the local authority began negotiating for the construction of a bridge across the creek.

Link to the Mainland

Temple Bar was erected as a cattle barrier across Winter Gardens' path. The wood was replaced with concrete, parts of which remain. Station Approach (where people boarded the late Frederick Hester's mono-rail) is left and right, but has now been redeveloped Temple Bar derives its name from that installation which used to be in London.

It looked at last as if a start could be made, but a number of shareholders who had made deposits would not pay up and this held up the operations of the company. However, all went well and the first part of the proposed line was laid and opened to Brentwood about 18 miles from Canvey Island in 1839. This line became known as the Eastern Counties Line and it reached Colchester in 1843. From here the Eastern Union Railway took the line to Ipswich. At various times branch lines were opened and by 1865, Essex was well covered and the whole system was controlled by the Great Eastern Railway Company.

From the travellers point of view the speed of the trains seemed fantastic at thirty miles an hour compared with the horse drawn coaches that seldom reached twelve. It was a good while before people would accept that it was safe to be whizzed along at such a speed and accidents were very frequent, and this did not help to ease the public mind. But like all new things the railway was soon accepted, thus more money for spending on advertising to build up the suburban towns that were once rural villages.

Old buildings on Canvey are confined now to a few cottages in the original village and to the two ancient octagonal cottages both referred to as "The Dutch Cottage". Of these one stands at the corner of Haven Road whilst the other is further West alongside the main Benfleet Road. They are the earliest surviving buildings on the Island. The Haven Road cottage was built in 1621 and its now yellow wash walls are held in place by iron struts. The other cottage though older (1618) is in a better state of preservation and its pink walls, blue door and neat thatch give it an attractive almost doll's house appearance. Formerly in private ownership it was, in 1952 given to the Urban Council by deed of gift, indeed the building is registered as a building of special historical interest under the Town and Country Planning Act.

The Castle Point Council decided in 1962 that the cottage should become a museum, it was opened by M. Van Enkelen of the Dutch Embassy in London.

The fabric of the cottage and its surrounding gardens are maintained by Castle Point Borough Council and the Museum is staffed and administered voluntarily by the Benfleet and District Historical Society.

Benfleet station, in the days of steam trains. The picture was taken from the pedestrian bridge which enabled people to cross over the level crossing when the gates were closed. Some of the right hand side properties still remain.

There are many exhibits which are changed from time to time. The fire irons in the living room are a set made by a craftsman over 150 years ago, and the old Tudor chair was found in a farmhouse at Canvey. There is a sampler on the wall worked by a Canvey child in 1819, also on the wall is a plaque taken from the old Village Pump which stood opposite the "King Canute" when the road was widened it was put in the Museum for safe keeping. Another item of interest is the wooden table where the literature is kept. This was made in the time of Queen Anne and has no nails or screws used in the construction.

There is a very old yoke, and as they milked sheep on Canvey and made cheese from the milk, this is an appropriate item. In the time of Nelson, wooden warships used to anchor in Hole Haven and members of the crew would come ashore to buy these cheeses from the various farms,

In one of the bedrooms there is a child's cradle and child's rocking chair dating back from the time of Queen Anne, in the cradle there is a child's lace bonnet which was made by a refugee at the time of the French Revolution. It was presented to the museum by a descendant of its original owner.

In the larger bedroom there are models of various ships that have passed Canvey. In a very large case there is panoramic scene of the River Thames and Canvey Island to Hadleigh Downs and beyond. Other marine models are a four masted sailing ship, made by the late Captain Brown and loaned by Mr. Brown of Benfleet. There is a model of Canvey Sea-front in which there is to be seen the old Chapman Light-house, this was made by my Grand-father Mr. John Fenwick, also made by him is a model of the Old Village Pump and one of the Dutch cottages.

During the construction of the new Canvey Road the then Secretary Society discovered quite by charge some old pieces of pottery and wattle used for huts, bones, a brooch and other articles which indicate at that point there was once a Roman British Settlement, possibly the Middle Ages.

In the gardens of the Museum is part of the first Canvey Bridge, in which was a swing bridge which had to be opened everytime a boat wanted to go through. This was operated by Mr. Harry Thompson who used to live at, "Hove to " Wall Road, Canvey Island.

Another claim, however, to being the island's oldest structure is the Lobster Smack Inn mentioned in the early chapter as The World's End and was well noted for many a prize fight. Dicken's in his novel 'Great Expectation' refers to the Lobster Smack and to its four-poster beds. The building today retains its weather board walls and is generally typical of much Essex coastal architecture.

Canvey has several places of worship of both old and new architecture. the Dutch had been the first to build a church when they came to reclaim the island. A place of worship was licensed by them in 1628 and built in 1631 in Canvey village. Little of it is mow built in 1712 it was rebuilt and dedicated to St. katherine. The church of timber, seated only eighty worshippers (the whole island population could hardly have then exceeded this) and was again virtually reconstructed before the 18th century was out. This church was pulled down and a new one built on the same site in 1845.

Also dedicated to St. Katherine, this little church largely of Timber and plaster, survives today by the roadside on the western edge of Canvey village. It remained in regular use until the end of 1962 when the new parish church of St. Nicholás was opened. St. katherine's consists of a small naive and chancel and is surmounted by a diminutive steeple. The church, which is now sadly mis-shapen due to the shrinking of its foundations, seats only about one hundred people. Architecturally poor, it does include several richly coloured lancet windows (including one that does St. Katherine) and a painted channel screen that runs to the full height of the roof.

The new parish church of St. Nicholas stands alongside Long Road and, though towerless, is of striking architectural design. The foundation stone was laid in 1960 and the church was opened for worship towards the end of 1962. Its striking feature is its steep-sided roof, the lines of which are continued down to the ground by buttresses on either side of the nave. Filling the triangular space thus formed at the west end is an area of diagonally set glass. The whole effect is dignified and fresh in concept and execution. It brings something of the Scandinavian look to Canvey and is certainly the most significant architectural feature in the island. The interior is light and spacious and enhanced by numerous items of fine craftsmanship. Of rare interest are two silk Bible Markers on the lectern Bible which were hand painted at the Torre Pellice in Italy.

Heritage Centre

This building was once the parish church of Canvey and was built in 1876. It was declared redundant by the Church Commoners and the Historical Conservation Society which was founded by Mr. Aubrey Stevens in 1977. Offered to become trustees of the building and open it to the public as an art and craft centre and folk museum. All the cleaning, decorating and repair work has been done by volunteers. The Heritage Art and Crafts Society has given tremendous support to the historical society by organising fund raising events to cover the cost of repairs, alterations and decorations.

Each year they have a number of demonstrations and exhibitions. the centre is open every Sunday from 2 - 4 p.m from June to October. The exhibitions consist of Needlework, spinning and lacemaking, painting, porcelain dolls at the end of the year they have a Christmas Bazaar.

Bus Service

After Mr. Hester's bunkruptcy the trams that ran on the monorail from Winter Gardens to Station Road, became unfuncionable the four times went back to their makers at Loughborough. Of them two were used at Llandudno for trials in 1907. Later the trucks were re-used and the bodies scrapped. One became a cricket pavilion. Later the only means of transport to take visitors to Ben fleet station was by horse and carriage. Around about 1920 a number of small buses started up privately a Mr. Knight, Mr. Hellicker Mr. Claxton and Mr. Nichols were a few that started up a private bus service. the Local Council Offices was then a house known as Fair Lawns, on the corner of Fairlop Avenue outside was a clock (Time clock) in the Long Road.

One of the very first bus companies on Canvey. Taken at Leigh Beck around 1920s with Mr Knight, the owner standing by.

How visitors used to get from Benfleet Statin to Canvey, long before any form of 'bus service.

These were two of my father's taxis, the first was in 1949 when we lived at Northwick, and the other 1954 when we lived in East Crescent.

An interesting view of Hotel Kynoch, which used to be on the landside of the sea wall in what is naw London and Coastal Oil WharveJs land. The hotel has been demolished.

If you thought the winter of 1986 was cold see what it was really like in 1929. It wasn't only frozen at Leigh, the Canvey- Benfleet creek also resembled the Artic.

All drivers had to stop and punch this to show they were running on time. In 1930 the Canvey and District Bus Service was formed Harry Titchen joined as a bus conductor in 1931 and was for many years a driver for his last 12 years he was an Inspector followed by Bill Windsor and Mr. Dent. In later years Canvey & District was acquired by the Eastern National Bus Service, it is now run by Thamesway buses, a firm based in Bristol.

Memories of bad weather

The Island was practically cut off during 1939 by bad weather conditions, the road was blocked from Canvey Village to the bridge by snow drifts, plans were contemplated to drop food from the air, but my Mother who was at that time at school in Southend said they cleared a path through the fields from the village to well beyond Northwick Corner which they had to walk, spirits were very high as everyone sang, tunes like whistle while you work etc., they had cleared part of the road to the bridge, the bus picked you up from the clearing, it was alright during daylight but very unpleasant once it got dark. My mother finished up sleeping at Benfleet Station, she was one of the lucky ones because she was at school with the Station Master's daughter. Another bad period when conditions were not much better was during 1945/47 when it seemed to go on forever, and again in the early 60's.

It can be remembered that during hard winters children could skate along ditches to the old village school at Leigh Beck. Also the lake at Lakeside used to freeze up. Occasions children and animals had to be rescued when they fell through the ice. The Croppenburg Canal, linked with the Island Farm lake at Leigh Beck never used, possibly because of salt water there, there was also a pond at Leigh Beck Farm, where there were plenty of skaters during bad weather, and plenty of fun during the summer months with home made raft's etc.

Ghosts

There has on Canvey been recalled some ghost stories. A Viking warrior has been seen to walk through the sea wall at The Point, a horse, is thought to frequent the Lake after a driver, his cart and animal disappeared in it. The haunted House off Denham Road with a secret passage going from the house under Benfleet creek to Hadleigh there has been many stories about this house over the years, it has been suggested that the deep wall leading into, the tunnel was used for hiding contraband. The house in question, is long since demolished, rebuilt and demolished again. Mr. Bishop the Scoutmaster lived on the site of this old Farm house. Mr. Bishop who was J.P. got the Scout medal for Meritorious conduct during the 1953 Floods.

With recent construction of the underpass road, which now avoids delays at the level crossing gates, now closed, traffic today moves reasonably smoothly from Canvey on to the mainland and vice versa, although drivers of some of the large vehicles still have to exercise great care in negotiating the steep and narrow High Street leading up from the waterside to the small village of South Benfleet.

In recent months traffic surveys have been made with a view to improving the Island's "life line" even further with an even better bridge as the one installed in the 30's is slowly silting into the mud. Doubtless with the continued rise in population and perceptible expansion of light industries on the island something will have to be done in the future to meet the new demands on this most curious bridge in Essex.

Eventually the old bridge was replaced by one to the West, another road leading off the Island from lakeside via Somnes Avenue to Benfleet, and The Canvey Way from Waterside roundabout to Sadler's Farm roundabout at Benfleet. In 1981 a campaign was underway to get a third road and bridge off the Island but up to yet no decisions have been made.

The Canvey Island Urban District Council built a further 362 council houses in New Road, (between Long Road and the Winter Gardens area). Already built and let are the first 231 whilst the next 131 are in the process of erection by the industrialised building system. The New Road site plans include the construction of shops, two schools and the Amelia Blackwell Home for the aged.

Other old peoples homes are 'Long View' at the Little Gypps, completed by the Essex County Council, the Beatrice Littlewood Development at Kitkatts Road and the latest of all, Wrackhall Court in Gafzelle Drive.

The Senior Citizens Day Centre at the Paddocks Recreation Ground completed in May 1969 acts as a focal point for Welfare Work for the aged on the Island.

These, together with the other homes and bungalows that have been provided for the aged in recent years, are sure proof that here is a community that cares.

Quite close to the parish church along Long Road is the rather older Roman Catholic church of Our Lady and the English Martyrs and one that brings a touch of the Continental style to Canvey. This building is indeed conspicuous with its white walls and its beacon like white tower capped with a small green tiled pyramid roof. Although quite small and plain the church interior preserves a dignity that is enhanced by the wall statues and the alter drapes.

St. Anne's church at Leigh Beck dates from the early years of the present century and is of little architectural interest whilst in Waarden Road, is the new Methodist church a simple structure church hall and was opened in 1962.

Schools

The first school built on Canvey was The Old Village School in 1873 at the Canvey Village. This was then replaced by Canvey County School in Long Road, and followed by Canvey Junior School and Leigh Beck School. Private Schools before the war were Kingsley Hall School, Miss Mitchells School alongside the Baptist Church and the Miss Kipps School.

Whittier Hall was used as a primary School for all ages at one time Post war. The new secondary school Furtherwick Park was built, and then Canvey School became William Read junior School, named after Mr. William Read the Headmaster of many years. As the population on Canvey increased it was necessary to build another senior school, so Cornelius Vermuyden was built and in 1980 Castle View School was built. In the last 20 years another three primary schools have been built, Northwick Park County Junior, St katherines Church of England Junior, and Lubbins Park Junior School. There is also a Catholic School. St. Joseph's Infant and Junior School.

A more recent building in Long Road is the Fire Station, which was opened in 1962. Contemporary in design it is one of the most modern in Essex, and its facade is of glass and coloured panels, the theme being red and blue. The Essex County Crest is a prominent feature on the front.

Also opened in 1962 was the local branch of the Essex County Library service, a modern looking building in the High Street. It has a main entrance wall that is of glass from floor to ceiling - most effective, light and spacious.

Housing, too, is modern in Canvey whether Council or privately built. By agreement with the Borough of Dagenham and Walthamstow (now London Borough of Barking, Redbridge and Waltham Forest) a large estate was built on Canvey to house the overspill of Dagenham and Walthamstow. Over 424 properties were built under this scheme which was completed in 1962.

Hotels

The Kynocks Hotel was built in 1900, it continued to operate as a hotel until the Second World War, when it was occupied by troops stationed in the areas, it was later used as offices for London Coastal, it was demolished in 1960.

The Red Cow (renamed the King Canute after the floods of 1953.)

The old red Cow, was a timber building it was situated behind the Old village pump, which was opened in 1889 when crowds gathered to witness the drawing of the first bucket of water, it was later dismantled and a plate was placed in the middle of the road. When the road was widened, the inscribed plate was place in the Dutch Museum alongside the old water trough. The Red Cow was the focal point of the community.

The Lobster Smack

Claims to be the Island's oldest structure, situated at the base of the seawall at the end of Haven Road, and one very well known to yachtsmen. In mid-Victorian days it was a scene of many a prize fight. The position of the Lobster Smack with its deep water at all times made it extremely inviting to sea pirates, making it a headquarters for their extensive raids into the surrounding counties of Essex and Kent.

The Haystack (Renamed "The Tropics")

The pub is situated on the corner of Furtherwick Road it was run by Madam French who was a charactor in her own rights, she was helped by her son Howard French who unfortunately died at a early age through eating oysters out of season. Many social events were held in their well known lounge, my grand-parents attended many dance and fancy dress occasions before the war. During the war dances continued regularly for the locals and troops that were stationed on the Island, my mother can remember the siren going about five minutes before the dance ended, and the air raid wardens sending them to the air-raid shelter alongside the mascot shop where they remained until the morning, and then going to "Cockle Jack's" cafe for eggs and bacon, she did not dream in those days that Ann who cooked the breakfasts would be my brothers Mother-in-Law.

Hotel Monico

Was built before the last war, was very popular with holiday makers, day trippers and cyclists, my mother can remember the foreman in charge of this building as he was a local . Mr. Wade, he was a friend of my grand-father who then had a putting green along side "Uncle Sams's Minstrels, very popular with servicemen during the war.

Canvey Casino

Built round about 1935, was a large amusement arcade, with darts, tombola's, rifle shooting, dodge-em cars, haunted house, big dipper and slides etc., Upstairs was a very large ballroom said to be the largest in Essex. Over the years had been used for many functions, choosing of the Carnival.Queen, Police Balls, etc., It was demolishes the early part of 1994.

Sunnyside Hotel

The sunnyside Hotel at the end of Convent Road, during the war the King's Own Yorkshire light Infantry was billetted there, after the war it was used for while as a Hotel. it is now the Roman Catholic School.

The entrance to Canvey Village (from Canvey Road) before the Red Cow pub (left) was rebuilt further back.

The Admiral Jellicoe

The pub is situated at the top of Seaview Road, it was built sometime in the 1930's it was the only hotel during the war where you could get a room and for quite a while afterwards, during the war Mrs. Jennings who was then the manager used to let the local troops go there for a bath, as bathrooms on the camps were quite unheard of. It has always been used for social occasions, meetings for clubs etc., Dinners and Dances, also Wedding receptions. The inside of the Public Bar was used for one of Dr. Feelgood's record sleeves.

Hotel Ozonia

Was situated at the bottom end of Seaview Road, during 1938 it advertised 60 Rooms and on the front, a special feature was the beautiful and varied mural decoration in the rooms, a one room flatlet for 2 people cost 31/6d. per week, bed and breakfast 4/6d. Excellent Restaurant, Dance Hall and games. It was built as a temperance hotel, and was financed by a lady of some wealth who employed a Mr. Ernest George Trobridge to design and be responsible for the building of the hotel. The south and east elevations of the ground floor were recessed under the overhang of the first floor. It was a large building on three floors, ground first and second, the top floor being built with dorma windows, attic style into the roof. the roof was thatched. It is hard to say if this hotel was commercially successful as the timing was so wrong with the advent World War 11, as Canvey being classed as an invasion area, visitors were not allowed. After the war the property was purchased by Lt. Col. H.P. Fielder, and was used to house people. It later stood empty until it was acquired by local council, it was used for housing and was then demolished.

Mr. Trobridge died in 1942. During 1982 an exhibition of the work of this architect was opened at the Department of Architecture, Headington, Oxford, where he was hailed both as architect and developer of timber framed houses, which were designed to enable houses to be erected rapidly and a half the cost of a contemporary brick house. He patented this in 1919. He built a house at the Ideal Home Exhibition in 1920. Successful if unheralded until forty years after his death.

Beach House. Agent for Crest and Heather China.

Offered board residence at this unusual building that faced the sea front, commanding uninterrupted views of the Thames Estuary Miss Rose Humberstone who was the proprietress also had a refreshment kiosk on the seawall opposite for summer visitors, my grandfather about 1930 had a model putting course on part of her ground. After the war Beach house Caravan Site ltd., was founded by Mr. N. Thoupos offering holidays and residential caravans with Electric Mains Water, Flush Toilets Bath Rooms Washing facilities, and Snack Bar.

Coxes Hotel (The House for Canvey Crest China).

Coxes Hotel and Cafe was built about 1900 it included an Off Licence, High Class Grocers, Drapery Fancy Goods, Patent Medicines, surgical and toilet requisites. The monorail which ran from the demolished cattle barrier (nicknamed Temple Bar) along which is now Somnes Avenue passing Tewkes Creek where the power station for the electrification was built, through the back of Leigh Beck, crossing the main road near where the Admiral Jellicoe public house is now. Then down Station Road, towards the seafront towards Mr. Hester's jetty. the line terminated by Coxes Hotel which was on the corner of South Parade and Dovercliff Road, where Mr. Hester erected an engine shed. Little remains now Coxes Hotel has been demolished, and a block of flats have been built.

Features of Canvey Today

World War II naturally put a stop to new development but many of those who came here after being bombed out elsewhere, stayed on after the war, so that the 1947 population figure showed still another rise to 10,030. By the 1951 census this had gone up to 11,255. Development since the war has been continuous and both private and council schemes have been pushed ahead. Not only has Canvey advanced steadily as a residential and holiday centre but its industrial growth first started back in 1936, has been equally successful.

BEACH HOUSE CANVEY ISLAND

An unusual view of Beach House with Cox's hotel (left). Beach House can be visualised by standing on the seawall by Chapman Sands' Sailing Club jetty and looking across the island.

URTHERWICK CORNER, CANVEY ISLAND.

COX'S HOTEL.

My great grand-parents, grandparents my mother and myself making four generations, at Cox's Hotel on the occasion of my grand-parents Silver Wedding also my Uncle's 21st Birthday

Canvey's first hotel, Cox's at the seafront end of Seaview Road. Now redeveloped.

Canvey Hall, Canvey-on-Sea.

St Annes Church, Canvey-on-Sea.

In 1953 Canvey Island, in common with much of the East Coast suffered severely in the East Coast Flood Disaster. The sea wall was breached in several places, much of Canvey was flooded and unfortunately fifty-eight people lost their lives. the disaster however, was but a temporary setback and not even the summer holiday crowds of 1953 were demolished. The sea walls were raised by three feet and considerably strengthened and the sea defences generally improved by the Essex River Board at a cost of over one million pounds. There is no doubt that if the 1953 tidal conditions were again experienced and indeed, if the water came even two feet above the 1953 level, Canvey Island would be safe from the danger of incursion by the sea.

At the time of the floods, not everyone was in agreement that the money should be spent.

On Wednesday March 4th 1953 the Lord Mayor of London, then Sir Rupert De La Bere toured our flood stricken Island, and handed over a cheque for £20,000 from his flood fund, to the then Chairman of the Council Mr. Fred Leach. Normality was returning to the Island, everything was being cleaned up, the Island Football teams were again playing, a Wedding took place. Then came a threat to Canvey. Sir Alan Herbert suggested in a County paper the Essex Chronicle, that Canvey should be sacrificed to save London in times of flooding. This was challenged by Canvey's journalist. "McCave of Canvey sends a challenge and tells Sir Allen Herbert he is wrong and to come down to Canvey to a mass meeting of the inhabitants, he ended by telling him Canvey honours those who died in the floods. A LIVING CANVEY ISLAND will be a permanent memorial to them. Regardless to say he did not accept the challenge. later that month a Coastal Flooding Committee was set up known as the Waverly Committee after the Rt. Hon Viscount Waverley who had visited Canvey during the disaster.

Those who died in the flood were recalled to mind when a mass memorial service was put on record for Mr. Reg Stevens, who was at that time the Island Council Engineer and surveyor, he was called from his sick bed in 1953 to take command, direct rescue operations and organise the mass evacuation of nearly 10,000 people in extreme conditions, he had been invalided out of the army nine years earlier, a major suffering from war wounds.

Over forty years have passed, and memories are beginning to fade, but I don't think anyone will ever forget the "miracle baby" as she was known, she survived the floods after bobbing around in her carry cot for 12 hours, both her parents were drowned. There was a humorous side to some of the stories, there was a friend of my mother's Mrs Gibbs who lived in Cedar Road, before leaving her house to go to relations in London, she put the children's pet rabbits in the upstairs bedroom where she had not long laid new carpet, when she returned she found the carpet perfect except that all the green leaves on the carpet had been eaten, the rabbits were fine. there was the lady who saw a Christmas cake floating away down the garden path. In Foster Road, there was a lady who had awoke about 1..30 a.m. to hear water gushing, she woke her husband, he got up and opened the door, water rushed in. In spite of being 7 month's pregnant, she managed to get over the garden fence to the house next door where they had an upstairs. They stopped there until daylight, her husband then swam back to their house, collected a tin bath, which she sat in and he pushed her along Foster Road, and Larup Avenue to higher ground. An army lorry then took her to the reception centre.

North Avenue Area was hit by the second tide.

My father who had a Tipper lorry was asked by the police if he would start evacuating some of the families that lived in Cedar Road, we lived in East Crescent at the time, he told us he would come back for us on the next trip, my mother was giving us breakfast standing in about a foot of water, and trying to get a few things together. It was not long before my father returned, soaking wet, evidently in North Avenue there was a dip in the road, the lorry with his passengers were going down and down, he had to get out, he was up to his waist in water and lifted all the people out including a lady who was eight months pregnant with twins. The lorry remained in that position for several days until the water subsided, it had to have a new engine owing to the corrosion of salt water.

A pair of oars break the cold silence of the rippling water Denham road. There was little to be said.

Canada Corner

A planting ceremony was held in 1962, by the Chairman of Canvey Island District Council, to resite the trees donated by the people of Canada, to Canvey Island after the 1953 flood, to a corner of the Newlands Refuse Tip, as a tribute to the kindness of the Canadian people. The Canadian Maple trees were planted by the Chairman of the Council Mr. George Prince J.P. Councillors D.H. Holdaway, George A Pickett, and Lt. Col. Horace Fielder T.D.

The Rosemary bushes were planted by the then Joint Parliamentary Under-Secretary of State Bernard Brain .M.P. (now Sir Bernard Brain) The Public Health Inspector Donald J. Legge. To day alot of the trees have been planted in various parts of the Island.

A luncheon held at Newlands' refuse tip.

In 1963 a Canvey island Festival was held, run by the young Socialists and Young, Conservatives, they invited the Chairman of the council and the public health inspector to have a picnic on it, the challenge was readily accepted, a lunch was prepared, and members of the Council together with visiting dignitaries including the Mayor of Dagenham and Walthamstow, Chairman Sid Alterman J.P. and the councillors wives.

In the heart of our Island, is a reminder of our past a lake which has also given its name to lakeside Corner which goes back to Roman times when it was an oyster-bed.

The Lake

In the heart of our Island, is a reminder of our past, a lake which has also given its name to Lakeside Corner which goes back to Roman times when it was an oyster-bed. When the Island was reclaimed by engineers from the Netherlands they built a wall along, what was then a continuation of Small Gains creek. The wooden sluice which was discovered, is now preserved in the grounds of the Dutch Cottage museum, this was mid-way down the lake, the fence remained until about 1935, the marshland and plants indicated of earlier salt water, most probably traces of red hills.

On the left of the lake was the Oysterfleet Club, the Proprietor Mr Mick Saunders being a popular Canvey builder, this has now been demolished and in its place there is to be a 16 bedroomed Motel pub and restaurant, completion is expected at the end of May 1995, the scheme is to be similar to the Watermill Hotel at Basildon.

This sluice was mid-way down The Lake. The fence was still there about 1935. Note the marshland and plants, indicative of earlier salt water.

At one time trees were planted outside the Canvey Council School in memory of Canvey Soldiers killed in the 14 - 18 War. They were removed when the new school was built, in their, place was built a War Memorial to the dead of the first World War, it was in Long Road, at the junction of Craven Avenue, it has since been removed to the Paddocks. Canvey War Memorial was built in memory of the dead in the second World War, the night it was officially opened, it was only a few hours that disaster struck, it was immediately put into use as a rescue centre as it was the night the sea wall was breached and many people were drowned.

Through the efforts of the late Councillor Fred Leach the farmer from Waterside Farm, and a devoted band of hard workers it was built in memory of the Island dead that lost their lives in the war.

Five Generations of Builders

London Cry
Built by William Fenwick

Reed House
Built by John Fenwick

Eastern Esplanade, built by George White

Benfleet Road, built by Brian White

Sixty Acres, built by Paul White

The foundations and steel frame of the proposed new hotel

Small Gains' creek in the 1930's. The ship (background) is the ANNIE JONES. The creek was dammed off after the 1953 flood

This old ship was moored in Small Gains Creek for many years. It was then in the part now dammed off. Before the last war it was used as a floating tea-room. When in use she was a coaster under sail, almost every child that spent their childhood or spent holidays in Canvey has at one time played on this boat

This is the houseboat where, Charlie Stamp, his wife Renee and son John (known as Winkle) lived, Charlie earned a living wheeling and dealing.

Shops and houses in the course of construction Sixty Acres.

LOBSTER SMACK

My mother when she was three years old on the Saltings with my Great Aunt Ann in 1928.

The Salting's never change this was at a Bar-B-ecue, in 1992 with my brother Chriss and nephew Jack Fenwick.

Shops past and present

The Original Canvey High Street was once a seawall, but when other parts of Canvey was walled up, it became a highway, being lowered later when it was rebuilt. in the summer months shops used to keep open to the early hours of the morning catering for the cyclists that used to arrive from London at all hours, either going to a Camp site, camp in relations gardens and even used to pitch their tents beneath the sea wall. even in the winter it was not unknown for potential customers to knock up shopkeepers after normal working hours.

Some of these shops were built in the most unusual places, in unmade roads away from the High Street, selling everything from food to shoes and boots. There was Brown's Stores which was in Zider Pass half way between Clayton's Farm duck pond and the steps onto the seawall known as Brown's steps. Clarke Stores in Bardenville Road, where unfortunately either the daughter or niece Joyce Clarke was run over and killed by a bus in Canvey High Street, there was a store in Hindle's Road run by an ex Naval Gentleman later this was known as "Amy's", Bond's Stores in Acadia Road, later moved to the High Street. C.A. Shayes was shop at one end and a home, also Iris Stores, Dolly Dennhards shop in Seaview Road, Lunn's Stores in Winter Gardens also a Post Office, and Cherry Stores which many years ago used to be a lending library, was a lakeside path. Most of these bungalow type shops have now been demolished and replaced by houses. One original shop still stands now, it is known as The Clock House which sold China and Glass, Drawing Materials, Guide Books, Fancy Goods, Toys, Boots and Shoes.It was also an Agency for Railway Tickets. It was later a greengrocer's called the Grannary.It now sells Bird Cages, Gold Fish and foods for Pets, now renamed Pet's and Things, it is in the High Street opposite Maurice Road.

A few of the old names still remain in the High Street, although their original owners have now passed on, such as Canvey Supply Company Ltd., most probably the oldest business on the Island, Jones Stores Steven's Bakery's, tower Radio which pre war used to let out babies prams to holiday makers.

Today it is a different story in 1977 demolition took place of all the properties in the Lakeside Corner to Knightswick Road, Canvey Clinic, Hoyl's Butchers, Barber Shop, Newsagents, Gift Shop, Altermans Shopping, Arcade Canvey News Office, Filling Station. In 1978 Essex County Councillor Ray Howard (then Castle Point Chairman) layed the foundation stone of the shopping centre. Today Knightswick Shopping Centre is a focal point on Canvey, it incorporates the new Somerfield Superstore, comfortable undercover shopping, easy safe and secure parking with on site security, it is the only shopping centre in the area presented with the gold award.

Each week a different exhibition or demonstration is held. During the Christmas period Santa Claus is always in residence with a colourful nativity display accompanied at times by the Salvation band playing Christmas carols.

There is an open market which opens Tuesdays Fridays and Saturday, Thursdays is a second hand stall day, where different organisations sell their goods.

The Barn Cafe

My mother Iris White nee Fenwick with her friend the late Iris King nee Pierce whose parents owned the Cafe. This was taken the day war was declared.

Before the war Canvey was a great place for weekend trippers, these places of yesteryear where you could get cheap accomodation, bed & breakfast. The Traveller's Hall, Leigh Beck, Mrs. C. Jones Proprietress Small Parties and Cycling parties catered for. Brown Store's. The Point Proprietress. Mrs. Brown Taylor.
Camping Ground, Boats for hire.

The Handy Shop, Seaview Road, Flats, Single Rooms and Tents. Proprietress. Mrs. Dennhardt.
(My mother can remember she used to sell chips out side from a stall, she seems to remember her teaching tap dancing as well). Iris Universal Stores. Crescent Road, Grocers Tobacconists, Footwear and Drapers. Bungalows for sale and to let.

The Old Barn Snack Bar. Part of Leigh Beck Farm. Proprietor Mr. G. Pierce. Barn 300 years old. Ices, minerals, spades pails, bathing costumes, rocks. A Camp site at the rear, cyclists welcome. The Barn was a very popular place during the war with the troops that were stationed nearby manning the searchlight where Halcon stands now, also the force's that were home on leave, it was almost like a N.A.A.F.I or Y.M.C.A always filled with Soldiers Sailors and Airmen.

Clubs

Were very popular part of life of Canvey, it appears that most residents were a member of one club or the other. There was the Premier Club where the shopping centre now stands, the Canvey Club, The Kynock Club, Bohemia Hall and Small Gains Club all in the High Street. At Leigh Beck there was "The Thur Daka Club" which was an orange building in the Point Road, near to Southfalls Road, behind "Peter House" which is now The Spiritulist Church in Point Road was a Tennis Club owned by Mr. and Mrs. King just before the war, this was aquired and known as "The Polish Settlement" providing holidays for Polish Children.

"The Rendevous Club" which was run by Mr. and Mrs. Went was in Larup Avenue. This club was burnt down.

Furtherwick Road, looking towards Lakeside Corner. The roof of the building (right) was that of a bungalow named "Castle View".

Demolition being carried out at Lakeside Corner to make way for the Knightswick shopping centre.

Clark's Stores, which used to be in Bardenville Road, on the bottom right-hand side near Small Gains' seawall.

Unbelievably Lakeside Corner 60 years' ago although the corner shop (left) is still there.

In the heart of Leigh Beck, Claydon's Farm duck pond, with a board indicating Brown's Stores the house in front of the bridge was called the "White House" where at one time the O'Dare family lived, also the Pierce family who had "The Barn Cafe" the house to the left was called "The Red House" at one time Mr. and Mrs. Turner lived there.

Industrial Canvey

Industries and two Industrial Estates that have been established with the aid of the local council, one of these is the Charfleet Industrial Estate at the western end of Long Road, in Canvey Village, which can be reached along the new dual carriageway from Benfleet, the other is located at Leigh Beck.

Canvey Industries include, Printing, Electro-Plating, Book Binding, Electrical and Electronic Engineering, Manufacture of Joinery, Car Repairs, Car Breakers, Boat Building, Clothing Manufacture, Curtain Makers and many more.

On Sundays there is a Open air Market, with 200 permanent stalls at Charfleets, a special bus caters for this and picks up along the High Street. An Industrial Association was formed about 12 years ago. At that time the President was Pat Jefford, Supreme Drapes Ltd, and Hon. Secretary Bill Droy, Photo Science Ltd, they instigated the name board that stands up the top of Charfleets Estate giving the name, Unit Number and Road of each firm. They now have a permanent Security Office manned 24 hours a day.

Close to the Thames Bank at Hole Haven are the Terminals, Jetties and Storage Tanks of the Regent Oil Company and the London Coastal Oil Wharves Ltd. Planning permission was sought in 1964 for the construction of an oil refineries. This idea was first supported by Canvey Council, but the plan was rejected by the Essex County Council. After a public enquiry and a Ministry finding for the refinery company, plan went ahead for plant producing two million tons of crude oil a year, but nothing materialised.

The Italian firm sold their stake in the refinery, to the American firm Occidental, there was a standstill from 1978 until 1980, work then started which only lasted 10 months, it was left desolate with tanks jetty and chimney, it was then put on the market.

In 1988 Mr. De Savary bought up a stretch of the waterfront including the Occidental site, plus another 1300 acres. He applied for planning permission for 4,000 houses, Business park, Shopping Centre and Parkland. This went to public enquiry. In August 1991 The Environment Department with Michael Hessletine at the helm, refused the scheme. Three years later Mr. De Savary after his previous defeat applied for a Retail Park the result is still awaited. Canvey Island has the distinction of being the first locality of any size in the British Isles to be converted to supplies of natural gas, since the summer of 1966 when the North Thames Gas Board successfully converted the whole of the Islands' gas supplies to neat natural gas from the sands of the Sahara.

Canvey still attracts a number of day trippers, and due to the Holiday Camps quite a few tourists.

Amusements and Recreations

Since the raising of the sea-wall, it means you can walk for miles on a concrete path on the beach side of the wall. Along the sea front the Casino has been demolished and in its place at the moment there are a few swings and a round-about. There are quite a few usual seaside shops selling buckets and spades etc and Amusements Arcades a Snooker Hall and a Nightclub.

The Island has no theatre, but amateur productions concerts and other social advents are held at local halls. These include include the George Pickett Hall, Labour Hall, War Memorial Hall, The Paddocks, Womans Institute, The Red Cross Hall and Small Gains Hall.

Small parks with childrens recreation grounds are numerous, all within the last years have been made safer. On the south side of the Long Road where the Paddocks stands, is a pleasant recreation ground which has been enchanced by the provision of rose beds, paths and skillfully positioned seats. C.I.S.C House, a day centre for the elderly is in this vicinity. King George V Playing Fields where once Canvey's Festival of Sport took place, which was organised by the Sport's Development Council each year. This was opened by a demonstration by Canvey Keep Fit Ladies, there was sports Football matches, comic and otherwise, tug of war sideshows etc, it is a large open space with 4 Football pitches, Tennis Courts, and an open pavilion.

Waterside Farm

Sports and Leisure Centre is a modern sports complex, it has a large swimming pool and a smaller one for children. There are Squash Courts, a Large Hall for Keep Fit Indoors Football or Badminton. Surrounding the Sports Hall are Football Pitches, a flood-lit running Track and Model Train and opposite is an 18 hole Golf Course. There is a Bar in the sports complex, and also one at the Golf course.

Clubs and Associations

Canvey has a strong community feeling and this is evidenced by the large number of clubs and organisation found on the Island. There are Football, Rugby, Cricket, many Boy's Football teams, Yachting, Angling, Weight Lifting, Keep Fit Classes and Aerobics Classes.

There are political clubs, theatrical and Dance Classes for children. The Georgette Juveniles have been part of the Canvey scene for so many years, they must have raised an awful lot of money for charities through the years.

Sailing is one of the prime pastimes of Canvey and the Thames Estuary and adjacent creeks offer superb opportunities to amateur yachtsman. On the Island itself yachting and boating facilities centre mostly on the east of Canvey at Leigh Beck and Small Gains and in Hadleigh Ray and Benfleet Creek.

On the Thames waterfront is The Chapman Sands Sailing Club this is a popular club for sailing and racing, they have a club house next to where Beach House once stood, the boats are launched of the old but repaired Cayton's jetty where in days gone by you could take a trip round Chapman Lighthouse. This jetty was built where the original Mr. Hester's jetty stood, which was used to barge ashore materials for the construction of the ill-facted mono-rail.

Hole Haven is another popular place for visiting yachtsmen, and racing as it always has high water. In 1981 a trawler race took place, when Sylvia Wood (Deaconess at St. Katherine's) gave a dedication. The event in aid of the Royal Lifeboat Institution.

The Island Yacht Club, has been in existence for many years, its Headquarters are at the end of Wall Road, Leigh beck, it is shortly to move on to the actual Saltings just off of Canvey Point. It is very popular club, and has always had a very flourishing membership unfortunately the Commodore Arther Rapkin who founded the club many years ago passed away at the early part of this year, a few month's later a flotilla of craft held a Remembrance Service off of Canvey Point when his ashes were scattered at sea. A lot of the members came from London in the very early years and bought holiday bungalows here enabling them to come for weekends so as they could take full advantage of the tides. When I a teenager I was a member of the then flourishing Cadet Section which used to sail Mirroe Ding's. There was a gentleman that used to come down from London who wished to learn to sail, my Uncle Jack Fenwick obliged it wasn't until a few months later they found out who hear was, when he was made the Chancellor of the Exchecqer Mr. Heathcooer Amery.

Tewkes Creek Yacht Club has a jetty in Tewkes Creek with many small craft, the Sea Scouts are always very active in this area.

Canvey Carnival

In 1995 Canvey Carnival will have been a prominent feature of Canvey Island for 70 years, Mrs. Mary Dallas has carried on the tradition which was started by her father Mr. Red Andrews, who used to have the fairground at the sea-wall end of May Avenue. Each year a Carnival Queen is chosen, she is crowned just before the carnival takes place, and presides at the events throughout the year. Each year there is a Baby show with a cup for the overall winner, beautiful todler's parade, childrens fancy dress and a Horticultural Show which is usually held at the War Memorial Hall. For many years there has been a carnival show presented by the Georgette Juveniles, there must have been hundreds of Canvey children that sang and danced in these shows through the years. On the final Saturday of Carnival week there is the grand procession headed by the Chairman of Canvey Council which winds it way around Canvey. there is always a good attendance of visiting Queen's from neighbouring districts, bands, majorette's and local clubs. Fund raising has always benefited local charities. The Fun-fair is always on Canvey sea front during the carnival. There is always a thanks giving service on the Sunday.

Cinema

Canvey's first cinema was run by the late Mr. Henry Pettitt, who had been a travelling cinema proprietor since 1905 in "The Old Bohemia" Hall, long since demolished, he provided such films as "Charlie Chaplin" Harold Lloyd, Tom Mix and other heroes of those times of the silent screen. It was always very lively especially when children had come in without paying, and were chased out in the middle of a film. In the summer air conditioning was provided by an old aeroplane propeller hanging from the ceiling, there were a few tip-up seats at the back, but most of the other seating was chairs bolted together, Lemonade was available during the interval.
The Rio cinema was built a few years before the second world war there was a change of films twice a week, and special performance for children on Saturday mornings, always a great success.

During the early part of the war the Rio being the only pictures house on the Island was always full of Service men and woman, (alway long queues,) some people unable to get in. The Rio has been a Bingo Hall for a number of years.

Canvey Keep Fit Class

THE OPENING OF THE SPORT'S FESTIVAL AT KING GEORGE PLAYING FIELDS

Joan Ralph, Joan Bishop, Cherry Morton, jenny Clayton, Maggie Talbert, Smiler, iris White, Rose Beckford, Anne?, Sylvia Sicklemore, janet Offord, jean Deane, Renee Warner, pat ?, Pauline Hook.

A Canvey Football Team.

Canvey Council - Canvey Football Club 1948

Five in front are: Bob Giles, Councillor Harry George, Joe White, Charlie Giles, Standing Manager Cliff De'Ath a Police sergeant Fred Smith. Solley, Hull, Sammy Lowe, Ronnie Brown ? Harry Gill, Bill Horseman, Thompson, Ted Hall, Georgie Brown, Laurie Blaney, Sia Land, Ian Pullen, Reg Stevens, Councillor George Pickett, Short Harvey.

Canvey Keep Fit in 1960 waiting for the Carnival procession to start, in Hole Haven Road, opposite "The King Canute."

The Distaff Club in the 1960 Carnival procession.

Canvey keep Fit waiting for the procession to start in 1970 outside "The Gold Mine"

Members of "The Distaff Club" in 1974, on a visit to "Olde Time Music Hall, at the end of Southend Pier, before the fire.

NETBALL TEAM - 19944 -45

Front row ? Botterell; Maureen Moore; Jean Devenish; Elsa Moson.
Back row Miss Pugh (teacher) Molly ? Shayes; Jean Bailey

The Canvey Cubs and Scout Troop attached to St. Anne's Church
The Scoutmasters were Mr. F. Berry and Mr. Bert Green, the Akalas were Mrs. Berry and Mrs. Beryl Green.

Memories Before the Development of Canvey Island

The first visitors to Canvey Island fifty years ago were certainly ahead of the influx which began towards the end of World War I. The land they brought from the declining grazing lands cost £1 a plot compared with £24.000 today. The main reason for this sharp increase is due of course to the land betterment levy which has given cause for it to rise at least 40% in the last six years.

The early tents were pitched in a large open meadow, flat as all land on Canvey, with no habitation between them and the distant sea wall, winding its way around the island's circumference. In those days the island was still virtually an enclosed meadow, green and peaceful.

Recorded memories from old holiday makers who have now settled on the island.

"I do not recall having seen Mr. Hester, the subject of correspondence in recent issues, but there was plenty of evidence of his ambitious schemes, including the pier and the tramway track with it's half built power house. The track ran from the Winter Gardens - which in a sense was the hub of his project and where there was the nucleus of a model village - to Small Gains Creeks.

Parallel to the track, bordered by rushes, the remains of a sea creek which at one time must have bisected the island and which Hester planned to convert into a Venetian waterway. At the Winter Garden and elsewhere were several picturesque bungalows of unusual design including a "Swiss cottage" reputed to have been transported from an exhibition. The power house was blown up during World War I, so it was said, in case invading German force used the concrete foundations as a heavy gun emplacement.

By that time our own bell tents had given way to a small bungalow, later to be replaced by a larger one and our tents were brought out only if we had a party or if we boys asked. At the end of war more visitors appeared in increasing numbers as the island became popular, with the oddest habitations ranging from horse buses and pantechnicons to houseboats, and it was some while before the standard of building approached the early bungalows of Hester's time.

Marlborough House was situated at the seawall end of Station Road, now demolished but the ground is still vacant. One of its attractions was a concert party at pre war holiday time, often an old time music hall singer or entertainer was on the bill, Rooms were also available. After the war my father often took passengers from Benfleet station to Marlborough House.

The 25th anniversary of the Island Yacht Club, when they held a regatta and novelty sports in Canvey Creek, two of the ladies pushing the boats out are Iris White and Nick Smith.

A street party was held at the junction of East and West Crescent canvey, to celebrate the Coronation of Queen Elizabeth 11.

Probably the first ever Canvey Carnival, back in the 1900's at Winter Gardens. The former Swedish bungalow (now demolished) is in the background. The event then was to celebrate 'The King of Canvey'.

In the early days travel on the island was primitive. When the time came for us to return to London at the end of the school holiday it was always necessary to arrange a few days beforehand for a horse drawn trap, and we youngsters were posted as lookouts on the sea wall for its arrival. As soon as it appeared we began our struggle with suitcase and hampers across the meadow paths, then along the sea wall and so to the road and the waiting vehicle. The trap with all of us aboard jogged along the raise straight road, which traversed the island centre and on towards the station at Benfleet.

The whole journey to the station took just over an hour if the tide was out, enabling the trap to cross the ford, but twenty minutes longer if it was in as the trap disembarked us some way from the ferry and the heavy rowing boats might be on the other side unless the ferryman had spotted our approach. The end of the war,however, saw a spate of small converted ambulance vans which quickly replaced the horse drawn vehicles, only to be succeeded later on by larger motors and finally by buses.

One of my favourite trips as a boy was to cross at low tide to Hadleigh Castle and the Benfleet downs, and often we would go to the point which stretches out towards the river mouth or to the beach on the southern side. The cockleshell beach was much then as it is now, but a few years before World War I a barge laden with barrels of cement had foundered off the old sea wall and the cement solidified by the sea still in barrel shape was used to make a causeway out towards Chapman's Lighthouse, which stood on the sand about a mile off the island.

Sometimes we walked along the sea wall to the Lobster Smack, one of the most romantic old pubs one could hope to find. Looking at Lobster Smack one can well believe the legend that it was a smugglers inn, an impression strengthened by the costguard station directly opposite, which was then manned.

Memories and Recollections of Leigh beck 1925 -1939

By Iris White

When my parents were first married they lived in London, and my father being by trade a carpenter and joiner, used to travel each weekend with his tools to Canvey where he was building a bungalow, he had already helped build one for my Grandfather in Wagenham Drive, (later re-named Chapman Road as the road was more or less opposite the lighthouse). I was born in 1925, and when I was six weeks old the bungalow was finished and we were able to move in. My father had then decided to start building holiday bungalows, it was rather difficult because they had to be cash sales, although a little later A.M. Clarke Estate started giving loans. On Canvey I led a very free and unsophisticated life throughout my childhood, there was fields to roam in, unmade roads to play in, you could in fact head over heels from the top of the road to the bottom with no one to bother you only an odd stray cow or horse that had lost its way. Apart from my grandfather's house that was named "London Cry" an uncle, my father's eldest brother had a holiday bungalow in Bommel Avenue, so at weekends when all the relations were in residence, we used to picnic on the saltings, swim off, of Browns's steps and when the tide was out we used to walk to the lighthouse and play rounders or cricket on the mud flats. I can remember when very young being taken to tea to Auntie Rosie as I called her, a friend of my parents that lived in what seemed to me a very large house, called Beach House on the sea front, the house fascinated me as it was full of ornaments and curios, to a small child the house and gardens seemed like fairyland. Four years later my brother Jack was born. I can remember going to Claydon's farm to buy the drinking water for one half penny a bucket, my mother would carry the bucket and I would push the pram. Adjacent to the farm was a small shop come dairy, this was run by Cookie, the housekeeper of farmer and Mrs Claydon, she was always dressed in a long white starched apron and cap, just like in the upstairs downstairs programme, I can remember rows of shelves with jars of sweets, so many that it was difficult to choose, if we could not afford the half penny to buy them she would slip us a sweet each when no one was looking.

'HOW PEACEFUL IT WAS

Quick! A stout for my horse

WHEN my father-in-law first came to Canvey Island it was to see about buying a plot of land in 1901: A man called Fred Esther was offering free dinners to each buyer so dad bought four plots.

He and his family used to come down for holidays in tents, but by 1908 he had a bungalow built and had retired. The doctor gave him two years to live if he did not leave London — he was then 58. So he came to Canvey on 15s. pension a week and died at 86.

It was either landers or pony-and-traps that used to bring you across the island from the station if the tide was out, or you used to walk across stepping stones.

The community had to make its own amusement and at that time a lady named Miss James opened her home up for people to meet and have plays and amusements on winter nights.

Time did not count quite so much then as it does today. One of our first single buses, privately owned, was travelling from Benfleet to Canvey Point and halfway throught the journey the driver spotted the Rendezvous Club burning down. He and the passenger got out and strolled across the field to look at it.

One day a carthorse fell into a dyke and his owner asked my employer for a quart of stout, which he poured down its throat. It gave the animal more strength and, with a rope and men pulling, he got out

We relied on one another those days and I can remember a bungalow catching fire. As soon as one spotted it we dropped whatever one was doing and the women would take a pail each, the men a spade and go and do what they could to keep it under control. Unfortunately we could not save that bungalow.

Certainly we are much better off financially nowadays, but there is a lot of good parts I would like back again.

I can also look back with a laugh when I think of the silent films at the picture palace at Small Gains Corner in my courting days. One evening the operator did not turn up so the proprietor went to operate and the film was upside down most of the evening. But there was more laughter that night than most nights.

(Mrs.) D. MANLY
Westman Road,
Leigh Beck, Canvey.

She also sold milk from a very large jug also butter and cheese. Although we brought water for drinking, the water for washing and cooking was collected in water butts after heavy rainfalls.

When Jack was about 2½ years old I told my mother that he was having a swim in the water butt, he wasn't swimming he had fallen in and was drowning, luckily they got him out in time. When we were older my brother and I, used to go to the farm on our own. Farmer Claydon used to sit in a big wooden chair in the yard, he would sit my brother on his lap, and he would tell us about when Mr. Hester used to live in the farm-house, it was his pet subject, but my brother was more interested in going to the cow shed, to see Nelson (so called because he only had one eye) to milk cows. We would often meet Nelson with his herd of cows coming towards us, waving his stick, when we were out playing and later coming home from school.

When I was five I went to Whittier Hall School, I was taught by Miss Nora Bromley, the day I started school I remember I was most impressed by the Helliker sisters they were both dressed the same in blue dresses, another person I remember particularly was Denis Lloyd, who when he grew up he devoted his life to looking after his mother, I remember he was a poet, I think he had some poems published.

As there was such a mixture of ages in one class, after much discussion my parents decided to send me to private school. For about 2 years I went to kingsley Hall Road, where I was taught by Miss Irene and Miss Gwen.

The school was approached by the arcade of shops near Maurice Road, I can particularly remember Mrs. Richbell who was the school caretaker, she also looked after us if we were not well or fell over and needed bandaging up. She was a very nice lady that had quite a few children whom I think she had to bring up on her own. She lived opposite the School so was always on hand,

I was eight when my sister was born, nearly all the wives and mother's on Canvey belonged to the Nursing Association, I can remember my mother paying a subscription at Whitter hall to Miss Steven of this association, it covered you for sickness and for a mid-wife if you became pregnant.

Nurse Morgan was the mid-wife that brought my sister into the world, the night she was born was a very windy night and unfortunately there was two mothers in labour at the same time the other mother was at Gills Avenue, so it was quite a long way for the nurse who was quite a large lady to cycle, the other baby was quite a well known character on Canvey, Charlie Neale Junior. I can remember Nurse Morgan telling me that night, she hated winds, as one night over Winter gardens she was attending a birth, when she needed to go to the toilet it was quite a challenge to get to the lavatory that was at the end of the garden, it was next to some geese, that was not helping, she managed to get herself into the toilet and all of a sudden there was a gust of wind it lifted the whole of the wooden surround off and left her sitting on the toilet in the garden surrounded by geese. I think if anyone deserved a medal on Canvey it was Nurse Morgan, she brought endless children into the world under some very difficult situations, with her bicycle and hurricane lamps.

As I was now considered to be growing up I was allowed to join different clubs at night, today you would have not gone out under those conditions, but the unmade roads were quite safe to walk in during the friendly darkness, with the glow of the hurricane lamp to light the way. There was Magic Lantern, also we had a practice night for a concert when we were put through our paces by Mrs George she encouraged us in acting, poetry reading and singing. These concerts were always enjoyed by the participants and the audience at Whitter Hall. At the Baptist Hall we had Christian Endeavour, and the Girl's Life Brigade when we would practice very hard all the year for the display which was held at the Casino Ballroom every year. The greatest problem at night, especially in the winter was the muddy roads, they had been cut up by coal lorries and were at times impossible, you had to find the driest point change your shoes and hide your wellies behind a bush,but make sure you remembered which bush. There were quite a few charactors living at the point, there was Charlie Stamp his wife and son winkle that lived on a houseboat in the creek, Charlie was said to be a smuggler.

When I was selling tickets for the Life Brigade, for years I had my regular customers, there were the two Miss Lee's they looked as if they had dipped their face in the flour bin, there was another lady who lived in Southfalls Road, who was a titled lady, but I cannot remember her name, it could have been Lady Taylor, she was always very heavily made up, and wore large hats decorated with everything but the kitchen sick, and then there was Polly who always wore a long overcoat and a mans cap, she lived in an old gypsy caravan in the vicinity of Kollum Road, I think she later moved to the Holehaven Costguard Cottages, in later years after the war there was Mr. Benson and Fag end Connie as she was called who used to busk in the West end of London, they could be seen coming out of Benfleet Station in the early hours of the morning.

Brown Stores was the shop where we bought most of our groceries, a store that sold everything from paraffin to a loaf of bread, alongside it had a cage almost as big as the shop itself, this housed a monkey named Jacko, I was told in later years, that an Aunt had taken me to the shop when I was about 18 months old, while she was in the shop the pram rolled towards the cage, and Jacko who had very long arms, put his hand out and grabbed the fur on my coat, they eventually tempted him from me with bananas. We used to put in our weekly grocery order, this would be delivered by Joe the owner's son, who had a trade bike with a large Basket on the front unfortunately Joe was subject to fits, and on occasions he would be found on the ground surrounded by groceries. Joe was an epileptic who eventually had to be hospitalised.

There was Stewart the Pearly King who used to ride a three-wheel bicycle. Until the roads were made up every-one had to have their coal delivered in the summer, although Bernard the Oil-man used to deliver parrafin oil summer and winter with his horse and cart, also we had our laundry delivered by Bill 3yron and his daughter Gladys.

When I was about nine we moved off of Canvey as my father had a job in Middlesex, we had let our house at Leigh Beck, but the job finished earlier than expected, so we rented a bungalow in Grafton Road, opposite the Mason family.

Margaret Mason and I became very good friends, my memories at that point were building camps underneath the Labworth Cafe, playing games in the Rabbit Warren in May Avenue, we used to make camps, have picnics put on shows for the little ones, actually we were practicing to perform at the Jolly Boys, and Uncle Sames Minstrels. We both had a sister quite a lot younger than we were, these two were taken everywhere with us we taught them to sit in front and clap us as loud as they could, my sister became a teacher at Leigh Beck School and Margaret's sister Hilda (better known on Canvey as Auntie Tilly) taught hundreds of Canvey children pre-school nursery.

The day Leigh Beck School was opened I was amongst the first pupils, I had two very happy years there before transferring to the Senior School in Long Road, Miss Vincent the Head Mistress spent many hours teaching us to dance round the Maypole, and getting the choir perfect for the Leigh Festival, it was a very happy school. Some thirty years later when they were raising money to build the school swimming pool, I became the Secretary and Miss Vincent the Chairman, it was the first Junior School on the Island to get its own pool.

I was also a member of the St. John's Ambulance cadets when I was about twelve. The officer was Ms. Bertha Wade, she had run the senior section for many years, she got a group of us girls together and taught us from scratch, she was very proud when we all passed our exam we all had new uniforms, grey dresses and grey felt hats, we were to go to a big rally in Hyde Park London, to give us an idea what was going to happen in London, we all lined up outside the Haystack Pub and Madam Frenchand her friend Kate Carney the old-time music hall artist, inspected us. We used to help nurse's do duty on the sea front during the summer months, treating minor cuts and insect bites etc,.

This year I attended the 60th Anniversary of Leigh Beck School, it was incredible the amount of people there that I was at school with, I'm sure it could only happen at a place like Canvey.

I spent the next two years at Long Road School, at that time I started Tap dancing classes at Kathleen Geden School of Dancing in Baardwyke Avenue, we used to learn routines and some times we would appear on the Uncle Sames Minstrel Show on Friday nights on the sea-front. At this particular time by best friends were Iris and Beryl Pierce from the Barn Cafe and Terry O'Dare daughter of Mr. Terry O'Dare a local toast-master and Showman and Mrs. Elsie O'Dare who had been a dancer. Terry ended up in Ensa during the war entertaining the troop, sometimes in the same show as her father, whilst Iris Pierce and myself joined the Army.

Memories and Recollections of the Newlands Area of Canvey Island by Pat Carter.

The family lived in North London and my grandmother was first told about Canvey by a neighbour who had bought a plot of land in Norlands Road 60 x 60 for about £3.00 in 1919. It wasn't until 1925 when my Uncle Tom came down to Canvey with his friend Joe Middleton, and found how pleasant it was. Joe Middleton's sister Ada then bought a plot in Munsterburg Road 60 x 60 for £5.00 in1926 (inflation). My first visit to Canvey was in 1928 when my Grandmother brought me down with my brother John, he was 7 and I was 5. We stayed in a house which was called "The Retreat" no. 12, Munsterburg Road.

I remember crossing Benfleet creek in a ferry boat, and catching a single deck bus to Chamberlain Avenue, It was the old High Road, very narrow with a ditch either side through Canvey Village where there were thatched roof cottages, a village Pump, the Pub was a wooden building called the Red Cow. All the roads apart from the High Street were glass. I remember a local farmer Mr. Cook coming round in the summertime with horse-drawn vehicles cutting the grass and hay-making. In 1929 Joe Middleton's father bought a 60 x 60 plot in Llandsburg, then my grandmother bought a 60 x 60 plot in Munsterburg Road in 1930, by then the price had escalated to £30 individual plots were 15 x 60 deep and the minimum was 2 plots, although I have learnt that earlier in the century some plots 55 x 60. At the outbreak of the war in 1939 a 60 x 60 was £50 in the Newlands area.

In the early thirties most of the Newlands area was country, we could see all the way to Benfleet, we could actually see the buses crossing the creek and proceeding along the High Road to Lakeside Corner, today this doesn't seem possible.

A gang of men used to be employed in those days maintaining the sea-wall which was only an earth bank, and apparantly it was lack of maintenance during the war that was partly responsible for the wall giving way at Tewkes Creek in 1953. One of the wall men as we called them, was Roley Day who had lived on Canvey since 1908. He remembered Newlands as farmland with cornfields, and grazing around for sheep and cattle.

I still remember Plumb's Farm at the end of Nordland Road, it had a raised area where the livestock was kept if a high tide was expected, Mr Day Our Highlight of the year was to come down to Canvey for the summer holidays through July and August, you can imagine how us children enjoyed it. We could roam around for up to 6 weeks, we were allowed to go across the creek to Hadleigh Castle. A favourite trip of ours was round the sea-wall to the point via Small Gains Creek and over the Chapman sands to go cockling and shrimping. Also a trip down a Shell beach and Hole Haven to the Lobster Smack. My favourite amusement arcade was Andrews on the corner of May Avenue and Eastern Esplanade, Newlands remained rural up until 1939. Where King's Camp is now used to be a cow field. I remember getting water in buckets for the cow trough which we used for washing, for cooking we used rain-water, but as things improved, fresh water was available from Clement Dairin Chamberlain Avenue which cost one old half-penny a bucket. Other shops I remember were Atwell's the Butchers Stott and Bubbles the Grocers, Venables the chemist and Hom's Bros ironmangers, also Yarworths the Newagents.

First building in Munsterburg

Extension (2nd Phase)

Summer picnic, a day to remember

Boating in the creek

Helping with the haymaking

Bungalow, complete
more water needed

For shelter in those days we slept in ex first world war army surplus Bell Tents which my grandmother bought for £1 each. Cooking was done on paraffin stoves, and also lighting was by paraffin lamps. Huts and bungalows were being built, and the sound of hammers and saws could be heard most of the day. Canvey supply were around in those days and I remember their horse and cart delivering various building materials. Their wharf was at Leigh Beck and I remember seeing the Thames barges delivering their timber at high tide. Small Gaines creek used to extend down to Hindles Road and Mitchells Walk. At weekends when the tide was right it was possible to get a boat over to Old Leigh, have a cockle tea at Ivy Osbornes and get back to Canvey on one tide. By the sea-wall at Hindles Road lived a Mr. Coram, he was an ex navel man, and used to do the trips to Leigh in a converted Life-boat. He also ran a small general store in Hindle's Road, the old building is still there but unused.

One character I remember was an elderly lady called Amy, you could see her most days pushing a pram along the sea-wall, on the look-out for bits of driftwood for the fire. Another character who we knew as Old Bill who had grandeur dreams of building a Mansion along Mitchell's Walk, but it was only a dream, he did make a start, but only the concrete piers were ever built. We used to keep a look-out for Jim the fisherman and many a fine tea was had from his freshly caught crabs or plaice from Hadleigh Ray.

I had some marvellous times from 1928 to 1938, during those years gas and water was made available to the Newlands area, and by 1936 my Grand-mother had a 4 room bungalow on the site. She settled on Canvey in 1939 and remained until her death in 1952, so she never knew of Canvey floods, When I retired in I came to live on Canvey.

Memories of my Childhood on Canvey Island

I was born on Canvey Island in 1933, I lived in a lonely house with no near neighbours, my childhood was a very happy one, I loved my home, I loved paddling in the sea, playing in the muddy pools, catching crabs and prising winkles from the bottom of the rocks, enjoying the country life as well as the sea shore.

I had two particular friends when I was about 6 years old, Marlene Bibby and Molly Bricknell, there was always so much for us to do, picking blackberries from wild bushes on the slopes of the sea-wall, where often one slipped down, amid yells of laughter, whilst trying to pick the big black ones almost out of reach. The joys of rising early while the dew was still on the grass to look for mushrooms. My friends and I had much fun playing in the fields after the grass had been cut, and the hay ready to be moved with which we would build camps and have picnics in. I loved playing gone the old barge "Annie Jones" proudly displayed on the side that was abandoned in Small Gains creek, now damed off, here once inside you became a pirate a witch and a queen all in rapid succession. Rowing was an ultimate joy, rowing a small dingy down the back creeks, visiting a friend John Stamp, known locally as "Winkle" who lived on a lonely houseboat on the marshes of the salting, near where the new Island Yacht is to be built, and having tea and home made cakes and toffee from his mother. In July we used to go to the saltings to collect sea lavender, which was known at one time as the "Canvey Emblem" and used at Carnival time. I had a fear of horses, perhaps because they used to wander freely down the unmade roads and fields. One night when my mother had tucked me up in bed I heard a clop clop of horses hoofs that sounded remarkably loud and there before my eyes was a horse that had put his head through my bedroom window, some careless person most probably my elder sister had left the gate open. As in most bungalows on Canvey we had a loft, the hole was in my bedroom covered by a trap door, very little was kept there, only forsaken toys, but my parents used to hide our christmas presents up there, so it became a favourite hunt for my brother and sister when my parents were out, it was quite dangerous getting up there, they would stand on my bed, then my brother would get on my sister's shoulders push open the trap door, he would the grip the rafters and swing himself up with much prodding and pushing from my sister, then with his help she would by devious acrobatic jerks disappear into the black chasm, leaving me alone, I was terrified especially when they come down and did not close the trap properly, there I would lie in bed mesmerised by the inky blackness above imagining witches and evil spirits floating down to snatch me to take me to some unknown place.

I went to Leigh Beck School, and had a very happy time there, I was lucky enough to pass my eleven plus, and Miss Vincent the head-mistress took me to southend to the Cinema to celebrate, I then went to St. Bernard's School at Westcliff, and for a while I worked in the office of Egen's Electrics whilst I was waiting to go to Teacher's Training College, I then emigrated to Australia where I married my husband Frank Robinson who had left Canvey a year earlier to work on research at Canberra University.

Memories of my Childhood on Canvey Island

By Bill Gower

Canvey Island in the early 1930's and before that was a dumping ground for barge loads of London's waste and refuse. Human sanitation was non existent, lavatories were a large bucket under a seat in a small shed located at the bottom of the garden. When the bucket was full it had to be lifted out and the contents tipped down a hole in the garden. Everyone had this type of toilet and everyone had a garden full of holes covered in afterwards of course, but you never knew where to make the next step.

Main running water was also non existent, the water we got was rain, which ran off the corrugated iron roofs, down a pipe and into a big galvanised tank standing on wooden stilts, everyone had one of these as well, this was our water supply. We made our tea with it, washed our spuds with it, washed our clothes with it and washed ourselves with it. The deal was to climb up and clean these tanks out during summer, we did this like everyone else and found a dead cat in ours, it had been floating up and down according to the rainful and level of the water in the tank and this is true.

There was no such thing as electric light, it had not yet arrived. There was no gas supply as yet and of course no sewerage. Ditches and dykes were all over the place to drain off the water in the fields and gardens, there was only one road made up, and this was the main one that started at the Canvey side of Benfleet creek ended at the Admiral Jellico pub at Leigh Beck. Onwards from here it was an unmade road usually very muddy due to the Canvey Supply horse and carts coming and going from the Canvey Point.

The buses were individually owned and operated independently, bus stops were anywhere a bunch of people gathered, which was usually at the corners, but the drivers would pull up if signalled to do so. These buses were very small and most had an escape door at the back, drivers would try to cram as many people in his bus as it would take and should another driver roll up at the same time he would get out of his bus and open the rear door of the one in front and pull some of the excess passengers out so that they could ride in his bus instead, sometimes there were punch ups over this.

People bought plot of land of fivers and tenners, ownership would change hands in a pub over a few drinks, probably a few too many. Most of these plots being used for holiday makers, some very odd dwellings appeared in them such as a real railway carriage, and old London bus, world war one army bell tents, metal circular shaperounded huts, old van bodies, anything which kept the rain off was good enough for the weekend holidaymaker to enjoy. There were four pubs, The Lobster Smack, The Red Cow (Now King Canute) The Haystack and the Admiral Jellico. The Jellico was a comparatively new building and very big.

At the Haystack corner there was no road access to the beach, then known as Shellbeach, there was a sandy track that people could walk along to get to the beach, in fact there was a very large wooden gate across the road to stop vans using the track, this gate being across from Fisks Corner. There was no Casino Monico or any other buildings at the Beach end, and the Esplanade as we know it today was all unmade with well worn footpaths of sand. But there was an amusement arcade on the corner of May Avenue the sea front end. This was owned and run by Mr Andrews and it was known as Andrews Fair, he had a few roundabouts and swing at the rear and the usual mixture of penny slot machines of the 'What the butler saw' style. There were also small trading huts around selling teas, cakes, wooden spades and buckets for the children.

On Saturday nights the Canveyites would get togged up as best they could and make their way to the nearest pub or social club wellington boots being an essential part of the dress, shoes carried in a bag ready to put on in the pub.

The hurricane storm lamp was also included for use on the way home, some by folk well and swearing because their lamp had blown out. There were six heavy duty storm lamps used as street lights, six for all the Island. One at the Jellico, one at Gains corner, one at Lakeside corner, one at Haystack corner, one at Red Cow in the village, and one at Lunns Stores at Winter Gardens, or sixty Acres as it was also known as. There was a lad employed by the Council to go round on his bike with a can of paraffin oil, some cleaning rag and some matches. He had to turn the lamps out in the morning, clean the glass, refill the lamp with oil and hang it back on the pole, at night he had to go round again and light them all up.

There was just on Policeman and his name was Mr. Peagram. he lived in the Police house come station, on the same site as it is now but his was a bungalow, he rode around on a bike and kept law an order without any help from the Law Courts. The Fire Station nearby was by volunteer and part time only, very often a rocket maroon was set off with a bang and all the volunteers would leave whatever they were doing and then rush off on their bikes to the Fire Station. The Fire Engine was a bit ancient but it got there towing a water truck for the supply of water, it was a bit of a hit and miss affair but the volunteers were solid enough. Quite a few Islanders were real characters, A chap named Arthur Read was well known for his generosity, he would work all the week and then spend all his wages on beer at the weekends, he would physically run across a field chasing a rabbit for his dinner. Wally Brown was another, he had a stutter and ran a tea shop, there were many others to make up the party.

The Council was known as Canvey Island Urban District Council and it had its offices at a chalet bungalow on the corner of Fairlop Avenue, the name of the bungalow being 'Fairlawn' there were not many councillors, no one seemed to submit any plans for buildings because people put up what they fancied at that time, but such freedom was not to last.

There were some estates of houses in progress. The Fisk Estate at Driveway and the Fielder Estate at Clifton Avenue and Southwick Road and these were considered to be the modern buildings of the day, some still exists. A general picture is now therefore explained and if you have a good head for imagination then you will have some idea what Canvey was like in those days.

On Canvey the Bohemia Hall near Gains corner still opened week for 'Pettits Popular Pictures' for the kids, this being a flickering film on the screen showing Charlie Chaplin in custard pie fights and other such ancient films. This was in any case a comical affair when the elderly Mr Pettit would be at the rear of the dark hall with his hand cranking the camera and directing the film over the childrens heads to the screen in front of them, sometimes the film would begin to wander off the screen to the extent that half of it was being shown on the screen and the other half on the ceiling, but the kids enjoyed it.

Perhaps the most distinctive change that year was the buses, the old one as previously described were being sold off or transferred somewhere else and the replacements took on a new look, all single deckers still, but rather longer and all painted the same colour of green. They were not new ones but we accepted them as being a good improvement. The bus stops were also put in a place of recognition, all bearing a 'Bus Stop' sign. In addition to this the timing was nearer the mark and more reliable. A new system to monitor the departure and arrival times of buses was introduced and it came from a big clock housed in a weather proof wooden frame on stilts in the front garden of the Council Offices of 'Fairlawn' on the corner of Fairlop Avenue. This position was of course actually on the main road and when the bus came to it then all the conductors had to do was to walk a few steps and place his bus time card in the slot of the clock, pull a trigger or lever and the time was then stamped on the card. This had to be done every time and on each journey to Benfleet and each bus had to do it. So if a bus was running a bit late on one journey, then the driver knew and would make it up on the next one, this of course made a better service.

All this change was due to our previously independent bus operators forming an amalgamation with the Hadleigh bus company owned and operated by a man named Bridges. He had a small fleet of his own that operated in the Hadleigh to Southend area, the Canvey buses continued to operate on Canvey only but it was a vast improvement and people could make bus connections easier.

This particular bus was a noisy old beast and it could be heard in those open uncrowded days at Canvey in fact from Lakeside corner it could be heard grinding its way through the gears when it left Leigh Beck.

One day it broke down outside Gaylards garage in Canvey High Street as it was on its way to Benfleet. The fitter Jack Bradbury, came out of the garage with a handful of tools to get the engine restarted and had to sit on the big front mudguard with the side bonnet up and tinkering with the engine to keep it going, he went all the way to Benfleet and back like this and in those days this was news.

Shifting on a bit more to 1932 this was a year of speculation about the Island needing services of main running water, electricity gas, and main sewerage. Being a long time ago it is not easy to say which of these arrived first, or for that matter exactly when. But what is quite distinctive to us youngsters of the day was the electric street lights when they were switched on for the first time. For some time there had been gangs of workmen digging up all over the place, and when the lamp posts were fixed they remained unlit for weeks until we got the news that on a given date they would be switched on. This in turn created some sort of a carnival attitude among the locals especially us youngsters, on the selected night we all gathered together and waited outside our nearest lamp post and waited. Suddenly it came on, so did all the others along the road, what a sight for sore eyes, the cheers echoed around the town, it was a night of joy. After this it took quite a long time to expand the services to the outer side roads, years in fact, but it got there in the end.

The next to follow was the main water supply, all of this took ages as well but it was not such a spectacular event and it seemed as if the island was being dug over with trenches everywhere, then came the gas this being the same. But the largest operation of all was the main sewerage, this was the last of the essential services to be laid on Canvey Island. This began with ripping up one side of the main road right across Canvey. Gangs of men dug very deep into the Canvey soil, so deep in fact that water pumps had to be used continuously to pump the water out of the trenches that the gangs were digging up, the trenches having to be shored up with huge planks of timber, and small wooden platforms were built inside the trenches as the men dug deeper, each shovelful of soil being passed upwards in relays on to the stepped up platforms and finally to the road where it was loaded into lorries and horse and cars and taken away, when the trenches were deep enough then a fleet of small cranes lowered the sewer pipes to the bottom where they were connected up for miles, it all seemed to go on for years in fact some areas never got it at all until proper residential estates were developed.

By no means has every change been mentioned in this tale of Canvey since 1930 but those you read about are some of the highlights, and there is just one more to come and which many people especially young people will know nothing of or even have heard about, and that is the Military fortress that was built here commencing from near enough 1935. Also, when describing this very great massive construction I have to bring myself in with the details because I was involved in it all.

It was sited tight up against the seawall on the far side of the now Fielders caravan holiday Camp, or Thorney Bay camp if you like, and rather a bit nearer to Hole Haven. Quite a lot of the sea wall had to be dug away on the inner side and then shored up with concrete and pilings and this was only a start. All the materials for this site had to be brought on to the Island by road and dumped in a chosen clear field at the main road end of kitkatts road, this being the nearest access to the site which was then one and a half miles away through kitkatts road, the Thorney Bay duck pond and many fields afterwards. So a small gauge railway line was constructed and laid all this distance, it was to be used to convey all the construction materials, there was no other way to get there.

In 1936 a bunch of my pals and myself got a job with the firm who were to build it, we started off as labourers and after a few weeks the railway was completed, the diggers arrived, the concrete mixers, the winches, in fact all the gear necessary to make a start, all this had to be dismantled and taken by rail to the site and then reassembled again in order to get on with the construction.

After about three months some sort of pattern was taking place and we understood that the fort was to hold two great big six inch bore naval guns pointing out to sea, in addition to this there was to be quite a few small gun emplacements such as antiaircraft guns and machine guns and also search lights, this will give some idea of the size of it all.

I am not sure how it happened but one day one of the bosses a Mr. Clark asked me if I would like the job of driving one of the locomotives, I think the only reason he chose me was because I could drive a car and had been seen shifting one out of the workmens way on one occasion, and he thought I would be a reasonable one to drive a train. Of course I was highly delighted at this and within a week or so my locomotive arrived, it was a German make named 'Arn Jung' in fact all the instruments and reading were in German as well. I was given a couple of hours instruction on how to drive it and then had to get on with it but being only nineteen years old I had the enthusiasm and interest to learn quickly.

As a loco driver I had to haul a train of small skip size wagons filled with ballast and cement and all other construction materials. The loco was a diesel and smoked a lot as it took the strain of pulling such a load but it did the job day in and day out. Over the next eighteen months I must have hauled thousands of tons of the stuff up to the site, it was a job I enjoyed and got a lot of envy from my by pals who where still labouring with shovels.

But this exciting job for me came to an abrupt end on a Saturdays when I fell from the top of a loading gantry and broke my leg so badly that I was out of action for the next sixteen months, by which time the fortress was almost finished, after which it was the occupied by the military. Within a year after I had started walking about without the aid of crutches and sticks the war started, within six months I was a soldier.

Six and a half years when the war was over, the fort was still here, so were the big massive guns but there had not been a German warship in sight to fire at all the time. Eventually the fort was demolished and the seawall put back to its original form, the remaining part of the Canvey landscape was also Reinstated back to normality. Anyone born after the war would know nothing of all this, that's why I have explains it all.

In retrospect that fort must have cost a few bob one way or another, and all for nothing. I don't know who paid for it, but I've been in the red at the bank ever since.

Bill Gower

Later, but still before the last war, the scene changes. There is a jetty where Mr and Mrs Cayton ran pleasure boats. Cox's had a floating beach cafe and shop and Miss Humberstone's cafe stands out well.

A fine view of Sutherland's fairground which used to be at the seafront end of Dovercliff Road. It has long since been redeveloped.

The other side of the sea wall, near the Chapman Sands jetty was the pier built by the late Frederick Hester. On of the barges used to bring materials in for his development is shown. When his schemes failed the source got into bad state. This is how it looked in 1914.

A picture from before the war when the cyclists used to flock to Canvey they had their own Cycle Park. The crowds were watching "Uncle Sam's Mistrel Show" who used to give two performances a day. For six days of the week they had blackened faces, and had costumes of black and orange diamonds and mortarboard hats, on the seventh day they were always recognized with white shirts, grey flanney's and boaters.

My Grandfather's Putting Green, which was behind Uncle Sam's Minstrells.

An early sea-front cafe in what is now Labworth car park. Their Kempton meat pies were excellent. later seating accommodation was provided with deck-chairs.

Canvey Casino on Eastern Esplanda, soon after it was built before the last war. The cars and vans illustrated will be of interest to veteran vehicle buffs.

This is now where the new paddling pool is. Before the last war it was the Glider Pool with little boats and a ticket office, left.

Looking along what is now May Avenue, from the seawall. Flats are now on the left and the Windjammer pub on the right. This part of the road was originally known as Rosewinkle Lane. This view circa 1925.

Thames Estuary

From the shores of the Thames Estuary very few holidaymakers notices the amount of merchant shipping that passes up and down the river. It is in fact, a revelation to many people to discover the insignificant forms drifting quietly across the horizon are ships carrying the world's produce to and from Britain's cargo port. The Port of London Authority.

The history of the Thames as a port goes back many centuries. The first settlement of people in the London area was near the site of the present London Bridge. A ford was established there making it the lowest point at which the river could be crossed. The centre of trade gradually spread both up and down the river. Whalves were built and anchorages extended, yet trade still expanded. Dock systems were added to the trade facilities, and in still more recent years oil terminals have been built further down river.

From the estuary shores passing ships appear as little more than moving shapes. At Southend pierhead a better view, approved still further by telescopes for use of the public. On the Pierhead Lloyd's signal station and coastguards maintain a constant watch on the passing merchant shipping. Each ship is logged, and special messages are often Morse on radio telephone between a ship and Lloyd's.

At Canvey Island, further up the river, the ships impress themselves on people much more, being considerably closer to the shore. Most ships are bound for the up-river docks, but many of the tankers end their voyage at the nearby refineries of Thames Haven, Shell Haven and Coryton, the tankers carrying natural gas come to Canvey Island. The Liquid gas is carried at very low temperatures in special designed tankers, it is discharged at Canvey, and taken to different parts of the Country.

When merchant shipping approaches Tilbury it dominates the scene. Large cargo liners, home from distant places by many thousand miles, slide past on there way up river. Huge liners embarks into Tilbury to embark their passengers. The trade in the dock has created such a demand on space, that new quays are bei ng built.

The Thames, however is more than just an available stretch of water on which the docks can reach. It is a unique river that could tell many stories of age-old activities of smuggling in days gone by. Along the main route to London from coast villages carefully arranged dumps for contraband in transit, and popular tales record numerous tunnels, hollow trees, empty graves and secret hide-holes in floors, attics barns, inns and even churches. Even today it is not difficult to imagine the times when small boats would lie up in such places as Holehaven Creek waiting to land their cargoes of rum, brandy, lace silk, tobacco and tea. Contraband cargoes were landed on the marshes and taken inland on carts constructed with false bottoms. The year 1773 also saw an event which caused widespread comment at the time when a notorious smuggler named Lazell (incidentally there is still a farmer of that name living on Canvey, whose family have farmed ground for many years) was charged with having been responsible for sinking six kegs of brandy in the creek. In the legal action the farmer on whose ground this was discovered claimed, that the contraband rightfully belonged to him as treasure trove discovered on his property, but he finally lost his case and the Customs house took possession on behalf of the crown.

Some places bordering the Thames were dangerously exposed to those of the revenue cutters. At Leigh-on-sea the cutter's crew kept a watchful eye on shipping entering the Estuary, and the Pembroke, a large man-of-war, was expected to intercept any larger vessels of smuggling. Besides the sea patrols the men on these cutters had to keep an eye on the marshes around Leigh, Canvey and Pitsea. Before the establishment of a Coast Guard station on Canvey in the 1850's many rumours surround the isolated chapel which was three quarters of a mile from the Lobster Smack Inn and sheltered anchorage at Hole Haven. A popular tale recounts it on one occasion a local farmer rumoured that his house was haunted by an evil spirit. Led by their well-intentioned minister, the faithful chapel-goers and other do-gooders, went to help lay the troublesome ghosts and so help their distraught neighbour, while they were busy attending to the ghost, another group of mysterious visitors were spiriting away tubs of brandy from their hiding place in the Chapel to the mainland.

The men employed in the revenue service, were repeatedly faced with what must have seemed on overwhelming task, very unpopular amongst the general public, and more than ever in danger of loosing their lives, it is a credit to these men that they carried on their task, when the odds weighed so heavily against them.

The creek separating Canvey from Benfleet is the haunt of wild birds and has a distinct charm both at full tide when the water laps the numerous boats along edge and at low water when these boats and the many anchored yachts are left high and dry on the soft mud. The Saltings and mudflats of the creek are the home of many species of birdsand during migration times it is the resting place for an even greater number of wild birds and water fowl who are in transit. Common and lesser terns visit here from mid-July till the end of August, whimkrel arrive during August, whilst many breeds of gulls, (great black backed, lesser black backed, herring and blackheaded among them) live here all the year round. Among waders that may be seen here are curlews, lapwing, golden plovers, ringed plovers, red shanks, snipe and dunlin, geese and widgeon come up the creek to feed, and red throated divers are seen, and at times even shags or cormorants come in from the North Sea. Rover birds are also seen at times and among these may be mentioned grey geese, greenshanks and spoonbills. In the spring the bird life is especially abundant and to the bird watcher, the marshes are then at their very best.

It is of interest too, that the badger is now to been seen again on Canvey. The once flourishing colony here, was wiped out by the floods of 1953 but now at least two colonies have been set up and nature lovers can again see this interesting animal - one that is almost entirely harmless to poultry.

The Sea-Front as it is today, the Russian Liner coming into Tilbery from one of its monthly cruises.

You can now take a good walk along the sea-wall either side, note the floating oil-rig Hotel past the Labworth Cafe, it was a fantastic site when it sailed up the Thames all lit up.

The Chapman Lighthouse was in the fairway of the river about 800 yards from the shore. It opened in 1851 when the Masters of Trinity House were asked to place a permanent beacon on the edge of Chapman Sands to aid seafarers in their progress up and down the river in response to this request the Brethren of Trinity House arranged for a lighthouse to be moored in the vicinity from 1847 - 1851.

At this time plans were being prepared for something more permanent, the result was something very different from well knowr light houses round our coasts. It was built completely of iron, it had a hexagonal shaped body supported by seven tubular legs which were screwed into the riverbed. The light tower was about 50 feet above mean tidal level, and had a flashing red and white light every ten seconds. There was small but ample living accommodation for the keeper and his assistant, comprising a living room, bedroom, kitchen and washroom plus a storeroom. A small boat was suspended from davits attached to the super structure which gave the keepers communication with the shore.

In 1951 to celebrate the Centenary of the lighthouse, the Island Yacht Club Canvey Canoe Club the Canvey Island Sea Rangers under the Leadership of Miss Madge Moore, both my Uncle, Jack Fenwick and Aunt, Brenda Fenwick were in this contingent presented a plaque to the Master of Trinity House, a sail past of craft of all shapes and sizes was televised.

For many years members of the yacht club sailed out to the Lighthouse Christmas morning, with a hamper of goodies for the keepers.

In the post war days of World War 1. it was a pastime for residents and holiday makers to walk to the Lighthouse when the tide was out to play rounders on the mud-flats, and all to collect cockle's and mussel's on the return trip to cook for tea.

Very soon after the Centenary celebrations, it was discovered that due to the shifting mud and sand and corrosion of the metal legs, the structure was in danger of collapsing, so the Lighthouse was dismantled, after over 100 years of service, in its place to mark the sands is a flashing Bell-buoy. During the late 70's members of the Royal National Lifeboat Institution built a model of the Lighthouse to raise funds for the Institution.

The 6 foot high model was unveiled by the Chairman of the Council, a model and the history of this important piece of heritage was presented to the Queen by Bernard Griffith the long standing Officer of the R.N.L.I.

At Christmas time a hamper was taken out to the lighthouse. This picture was taken on the morning of December 25, 1954. Shown (back) Charles Neale, junior, Ken Gordon. In front, two lighthouse keepers, Bernard Griffith and Teddy Cayton. Member of the Island Yacht Club regularly made the trip until the lighthouse was taken down. It was in 1951 the Canvey appeared on television when the yacht club and Canvey Canoe Club celebrated the Chapman's centenary with presentation of a plaque.

On the 15th May 1954 her Majesty Queen Elizabeth 11 returned to the United Kingdom from her successful Commonwealth tour. The Queen was in the Royal Yacht H.M. Britannia escorted by the Daring class ships, Duchess and Decoy. Midway between Shoeburyness and the Isle of Sheppy they parted company with the Royal Yacht. The escort was taken up by four past patrol boats. As her Majesty came up river towards Canvey Island a 21 gun salute was fired from Sheerness. At Southend they were joined by Trinity House vessel a Port of London vessel and three Metropolitan police launches.

Meanwhile at Canvey, crowds of people thronged the newly finished sea wall. It was a grandstand for this stirring event, people seem to come from everywhere, some had even camped out all night, extra police had been called into control the crowds, traffic wardens of Canvey acted as guides to reserved parts of the sea-wall for school children and old age pensioners. There were hundreds of boats out on the water for the occasion. As the Royal Yacht approached Canvey Island's own flotilla of light craft went out. They were proudly led by Commodore Arthur Rapkin of the Island Yacht Club. As the Royal Yacht passed the Labworth Cafe decorated with a "Welcome Home" message from the Labworth flat roof, Canvey Sea Scout leader Vic Ellis, flashed out a signal, the sea scouts formed a guard of honour as the message was acknowledged from the Royal Yacht. The message sent out was "To The Royal Yacht Britannia. Welcome Home and Loyal greetings from the people of Canvey Island.

Canvey Lifeguards

Canvey Lifeguards Club was formed in 1958 under the instigation of Charles Carey. He trained with the Serpentine Lido Lifeguards in London. He was on the Leigh Beck Swimming Pool committee, when money was raised to erect a swimming pool at the school, the club used to train at Rayleigh Sweyne School, but as transport was difficult they applied to Furtherwick Park School, this was granted and they trained on Friday evenings. Mr. Carey also also taught swimming at night classes at the school. They also began a teaching programme at Waterside Farm swimming pool with over 150 youngsters being taught water safety every Friday night.

The Canvey Lifeguard also taught at Runnymede Pool, Benfleet.

The Club's first boat was a canvas dingy presented by G. Prout and Sons, and they were allowed to use the St. John's Ambulance hut on the sea front. In 1961 Bill Adam's organised a fund to raise money for the club's first rescue boat named "Island Gift". It was launched by Deputy Lord Lieutenant of Essex Brigade Shenstone, within days the boat had saved two lives. In 1970 they had their own Clubhouse and Boatshed on the sea-wall, that summer 21 children were rescued, and as the years went on they changed their boats for more substantial rescue boats. They had a very good liaison with the police and coastguards. For many years the Canvey Lifeguards, through their training programme have attained the highest number of life-saving awards in the country, and have held the branch trophy for this. The club has also been awarded the Lord Lieutenant's Trophy for "Rescue of the Year" at least four times.

In 1984 H.R.H. Princess Margaret was invited to see the Flood Barrier in Benfleet creek, and to see the new seawall defences since the 1953 floods. Her previous visit had not taken her further than Benfleet when with the Queen Mother, they had come to console the survivors at Shipwright's School were families had been taken for food and dry clothing.

The princess visited Waterside Farm Sports centre accompanied by The Castle Point Chairman Mr. Peter Woods and the Chairman of recreation and amenities Councillor Jim Bowden she also visited Canvey Point industrial site where she was presented with a bouquet by 13 year old Julia Hall when she launched a boat made by Prout Catamaran Ltd. The Princess was presented to the Chairman of the company Mr. Rodney Hall and other directors of this world wide known Company. the Princess went to various parts of the Island where during a walk about she met local children.

Saga of successes and Achievements of residents of Canvey Island at national levels

Mr Mather

Mr. Mather who founded a mission for seaman, lived on Canvey many years ago, he was also an author.

Miss Clara James

An Island pioneer who in 1909 opened a Rest Home for the benefit of over-worked and overstrained working girls from the east end of London at Lakeside, making it possible for many under-privilege young women to enjoy a Canvey holiday. In later years it became a family holiday centre. During the winter it was used as a social club.

Miss James was involved in many things, she began girls clubs in the East End of London, she averaged an attendance of 300 girls a week throughout her six clubs where girls were taught to a standard of gaining a diploma in drill enabling them to teach at the London County Council evening school. She was also involved with The Dagenham Girl Pipers, advising on their marching, they performed all over the world.

Miss James took on Factory workers referring them to what she considered bad working conditions and unhealthy workrooms. She became the first woman elected to the London Trades Council giving an account on a Royal Commission of Labour to the House of Commons. This achieved that woman inspectors were appointed to factories.

Miss James in later years lived herself on Canvey, she became a member of Canvey Council, a JP and a school manager, she was a founder member, president and trustee of Canvey's Woman Institute, she was also involved with the late Nursing Association. She attended and involved herself with 1st Canvey Girl's life Brigade, attending displays at the Canvey Casino, my mother can remember her presenting her with a silver medal she won for drill on of these occasions. Miss James herself had achieved gold medals one an diplomas from the British College of Physical Education and the and National Society of Physical Education.

The Girl's Bungalow was on the northern side of The Lake and provided holidays for London girls who otherwise would not have had a vacation. Now demolished it was run by the late Miss Clara James, JP.

The Late Mr. Henry Pettitt.

Was an Author and a poet. During World War One he wrote a review for the 34th Division and played in "Chu Chin Chow".

Lt. Col. Horace Fielder

Saga Of Success

Canvey has had it share of people who have helped put Canvey on the map nationally, who better to start than Lt. Col. Horace Percy Fielder, Councillor, builder, soldier, civil engineer and in pre and post days a developer, who always had great faith in the area. He was born 1906, joined his late mother Mrs. S. Fielder in their building business. He formed a section of a pre-war Territorial Unit from employees of Fielders Estates, the 192 (Essex) Heavy Battery, by 1939 he had been promoted to Lieutenant. In August 1939 he was mobilised for military Service as World War 11 was anticipated. During the pre-war years he was Chairman and vice-chairman for three years, of Canvey Urban District Council, chairman of the finance committee for three years, chairman of the public health and town planning for years, he took part in many local organisations. In May 1940 he was sent oversea to North West European Forces and took Canvey Troops to Norway. The Islanders were amongst the first to engage the triumphant German forces. France had surrendered, and he returned to the United Kingdom, the same month along with the Canvey Soldiers he went to Iceland as the Officer commanding the advance party. There he dealt with the Icelandic Government for the supplying of materials for the installation of heavy guns, and acquiring land for gun and camp sites. In 1940 he was promoted to Captain, and in 1941 was in command of 1,000 men building an airport, in 1942 he became deputy fire commander, Rykjavick Fire Command. He became a battery commander on the forth, and later officer commanding troops Grammond Island.

In December 1944 he became a General Staff Officer in the Allied Control and joined 21 Army Group, British Liberation Army (later known as British army on the Rhine).

In August 1945 he was promoted to Lieutenant Colonel. His last appointment was when he formed the Ruhr Housing Office North Rhine and Westphalia Ruhr District. Here he achieved national recognition and fame for his work. He was awarded the Territorial Defence decoration for his service to King and Country.

In 1947 he returned home to Canvey, he was once again elected to the council and held the position of chairman for several years. Among the many things he pioneered was the start of the access area scheme, in refuse he pioneered the weekly refuse collection service of today from the open bins at the top of each road.

It was in 1950 that Col Fielder launched the scheme which made him a household name in holidays circles throughout England. The Thorney Bay Beach Camp was launched, part of the camp was the Fort and Barracks to where Col. Fielder was first posted at the start of the war. It was a low priced camp but with all the attractions and amenities of more high priced camps, the camp flourished and became a working man's Riviera. At first it was limited to Camping and chalets it became larger when caravans and trailers were added, then an abundance of modern holiday homes. An full entertainment programme was provided this would consist of film shows for children and adults twice weekly. Georgett's Juveniles concert party, children's talent Competition, and Bobbie Bean's famous band show, Paul Casper a local entertainer Punch and Judy show, Canvey and Rayleigh's Brass bands. There are many Canvey children that can remember being chased by Col Fielder with his cane, who had tried to sneak in.

In 1952 he married his Secretary 24 year old Miss Barbara Fuller daughter of the councillor Arthur Fuller and Mrs. Fuller. His engagement was announced publicly in 1952 when he was defeated at Canvey's first own Essex County Council election, previously Canvey had shared a seat. Mr. Arthur Mason took the seat for Labour. At the counting of the votes Col Fielder created a national sensation by saying he had lost an election but gained a wife. He was married at the then St. katherine's Church in military uniform. The local Conservative Club was named after him as a tribute.

Mrs. Fielder was presented to the Queen and Prince Phillip at Buckingham Palace in 1958. Col Fielder had been presented to the then Royal Family at a pre-war level.

Mr. McCave and Family

The Canvey Chronicle

The Canvey Chronicle was the Islands's longest running pre-war local newspaper. It was founded and edited by the late Bertram McCave who ran it from 1931 till his death in 1937. Thereafter it was published until the war broke out in 1939 by the late Mrs. H.V. McCave. Then it had to cease publication owing to defence regulations.

In its earlier years a weekly feature was a cartoon from the gifted pen of the late Phil Blanchard, who also doubled as a reporter under the name "The Jackass", the drawings were almost always of local happenings, many of them related to the council chambers, today he would have had a hay-day. They were not always appreciated, however the artist did not hesitate to include himself, even the young Fred and Will were included.

During the war my mother, who was in the army was in the Station Railway waiting room in Preston, Lancashire when she picked up a paper, she was surprised to read a long article on young girl's point of view regarding bringing in a curfew. The journalist being Fred McCave of Canvey Island.

After the war Fred McCave was well known as a journalist, produced Canvey & District News, always on his bicycle, always first on the scene, nick-named on Canvey as "Scoop", if mobile phones had been available then I expect Canvey would have got more linkage in the Nationals. Fred then went on to bring out a District Community Magazine "The Bulletin", which was published by Riverside Printers, these were printed for about 4 years. He then published "The History of Canvey" and Picture Postcards of Canvey, these are now out in print.

I can remember when I first opened the Bookshop in Lionel Road, Bill McCaves daughter Lesley who was then about 10 years won a competition nationally run by W.H. Smith for short stories.

Mrs. Brenda Robinson nee Fenwick with daughter Vicky Robinson in the model Village on the sea-front.

My grandparents with my grandfather's younger brother Harry Fenwick and some of his models under construction.

My brother Chriss and cousin Janet on the Model Village.

Mr. John Fenwick

It was in May 1948 Lieut. Col Horace Fielder opened a history of Canvey in miniature, in the grounds of which was then "The Mascot Gardens, Furtherwick Road. The designer of old Canvey was Mr. John Fenwick there were replicas of the old Village pump, The Red Cow. The Lobster Smack, St. Katherines Church complete with organ playing, The Catholic Church models of the ruins of Hadleigh Castle, with the railway lines in front, with an electric train running when ever people were viewing. His first venture was in about 1929 when he had a model putting Green next to Beach House and Sutherland's Fair. He later had miniature golf at the labworth Car Park, and when the Casino first opened he had moving models of "World War 1". Before the second world war there was a model he made outside "The Mascot" where people could put coins in for the hospital fund. He also painted quite a few pictures of Old Canvey, some are in "The Heritage Centre" and some of his models are in the Dutch Museum. In 1973 he was still developing talents, he started making sculptors from driftwood found on Canvey beach, he was not only making money from American buyers, but a reputation among London Art Galleries. His work was accepted from the Marine Art, Exhibition. The model village attracted thousands of visitors each season, also school parties, he made replicas for other seaside resorts, including Isle of Wight, Clacton and Cromer. He also had a model exhibition in the Festival of Britain, and a model of The Battle of Tewksbury at Tewksbury.

Mr Fenwick died in 1978, his grand-son Brian White took over the Village but unfortunately the first week-end it was opened it was vandalised. Mr. Aubrey Stevens and friend of Mr. Fenwick said "The village was always a target for vandals" but John never worried when the buildings were smashed. He just built them up again.

Mr Geof Prout

Mr. Geof Prout was an Author who wrote amongst things, books on scouting when he often mentioned Canvey Island, my mother can remember when she was a small child, Mr. Prout having a sailing boat called "The Black Cat" which in 1930 Mr. Prout and my grandfather sailed from Canvey Point to Devon, she can remember seeing them off in the early hours of the morning, carrying the gear and food for the journey in her brother's pram, little did they realise that thirty years later, the same baby would be delivering boats all over the world for them. Mr. Prout was an officer in the Army during World War 11.

The firm G. Prout and Sons, was started in 1953 by Mr. G. Prout a keen yachtsman who decided to build a folding dinghy, which was light and could easily be taken aboard a yacht.

The folding dingy was tried out by his sons Roland and Francis on a duck pond, and it was found to serve its purpose perfectly. In 1937 Mr. Prout started building the dinghy's for sale and the family business had started.

The war intervened and all the family joined the service's and the boat building was temporarily shelved. After the war the business was restarted in a small barn which served as a factory. From then the firm grew, in 1955 a Limited Company was formed, in 1957 a new and very large factory had to be built, to accommodate the increased production of folding boats and canoes, these folding boat and canoes were beginning to be well known all over England. Both the sons Francis and Roland represented England in the canoeing section of the Olympic games in 1948.

In 1947 Roland and Francis thought of a new market for their canoes. Why not join the two of them together and use them as a single catamaran just as the Hawaians once did. And so their first catamaran was made, with the help of planks. It weighed about 150 lbs just under eleven stone all up, and measured 16ft.6 ins by 6ft maximum beam a foot narrower than the present model. Each hull was 20 ins across.

This pro type catamaran carried a single lugsail, a rudder and a dagger plate amidships. She sailed quite well to windward, and though she was slow in tacking, the Prout brothers felt that the idea was worth pursuing. Two years later, the Prouts produced their second catamaran, this time the canoes were joined together with bamboo poles, instead of planks, whereby a tremendous saving in weight, for the whole new craft weighed no more than 80 lbs. Catamaran number two carried a lugsail main and a jib of an International fourteen foot dingy. The hulls were 17ft. 3 in and went as fast as a dingy on beat, and very much faster on a reach.

By now Francis and Roland knew they must be on a winner. But there was still one difficulty to be overcome, it was rather to heavy to handle, and too wide to travel by road unless she was first dismantled. So it went back to the drawing board. The answer was finally arrived in 1956 it was named Shearwater 111, she proved so popular that 150 were sold during the first twelve months.

The Prout brothers went on to design and build many large catamarans, in 1960 they had an order from Van Opel the German car manufacturer, this was skippered from Canvey Island to France by Jack Fenwick, it had BBC and ITV coverage at Canvey Island, Gibraltar and France, as it was the first Catamaran to sail the Bay of Biscay. Another large Catamaran "Show Goose" was built for Don Robertson, he has won many times round the Island race, and holds the all time record for the fastest around the Isle of Wight. Snow Goose was taken by Don Robertson in the first Round Britain race and came second on elapsed time.

Prouts famous working boats are now used in all parts of the world. The smaller boats now being manufacted are the Scoobeedoo, Puffin Pacer and the Puffin which can be handled by children, and was recently seen on ITV Children's programme "Blue Peter". Sail Training Instructions chose her for use at Drake's Island, Plymouth Sound, and the army sail her through London's Tower Bridge as part of their initiative training programme.

Prout Catamarans was the only british boat building company building to the exact standards of Quality Assurance monitored by Lloyd's of London. This means that every part used in building a catamaran, from ordering it to fitting it, has been traced and carefully, monitored, the monitoring is constant, on the spot checks can be carried out at all times. The firm had built 4,000 cats and have won the Queens award for industry for Export in 1989. Many buyers sail their purchase from the U.K. or it is delivered by Jack Fenwick. The Atlantic is crossed 10 times more often by Prout Catamarans than other cruising cat. Their award was well timed coinciding with the 40th anniversary of the company, and moving to their new Factory on the Charfleets Industrial site. Mr. Rodney Hall is now the chairman.

PUFFIN UNDER POWER

King's Holiday Camp

Councillor Jack King

In the Newlands area a new holiday camp opened in 1956, it started off as camping site by Canvey Island Urban District Council, with hazel and Peter mason as the wardens. In 1958 it was acquired by the late Mrs. Joan King and Mr. Jack King when it became Newlands Chalet and Caravan Park, you could book continental chalets or a luxurious modern 4 - 6 berth caravan. When I was a student I used to work in the bar during the holidays, it was very popular with teenagers, my young brother Chris ran the junior disco along with Linda King where only soft drinks were sold. Chris was also the Lifeguard at the Swimming Pool. Over the years it has given a lot of students holiday work on Canvey. Many youngsters could be seen standing at the bus-stop nearest to the camp with assortments of prams and barrows etc, hoping to earn a shilling carrying cases. At the camp there was a Bingo Hall, Amusement Arcade, Foodstore, Snack Bar, Cafeteria, Turf Accountant, Boating Lake, also open all year round was the King's Country Club where one had to become a member, there was dancing nightly to top bands, many top entertainers have appeared at the club, many club dinners, Boxing events, choosing of Carnival Queens, open air events have included swimming competitions, boot sales, donkey derby's and Bungee jumping. Mr King became a councillor Jack King is very well known to Canvey Old Age Pensioners, as each Christmas he has given them a Christmas dinner. About 18 years ago he set a project for art students to design a Christmas Nativity Float, the winner's was copied, made used to raise money for under privileged children and Children's Homes, it is now a familiar site being pulled up and down Canvey Streets carrying Santa Claus with his sack of toys, Christmas carols being played over the loud speaker with its merry band of collectors, during the run up to Christmas.

Katie Mallet

Katie Mallet is our Community writer for Canvey Island in the Evening Echo, for which she does a very good job giving coverage on all the local events, from the Heritage Centre, Womans organisation to local schools. She is a well known Poetress who seems to be able to produce a poem, whatever the event, be it a season for the year, children going back to school or breaking up for

Summer holidays, a joyful happening or a disaster at a drop of a hat. She has often been heard on the radio, and has had poems accepted and printed. She is a member of the Southend Poetry Society.

Geof Barsby

Publisher of "The District News, and Author of the book "Canvey Island".

Olivia Whitcombe

Wrote a book on The History of Canvey called "The Invaders, dedicated to her late father Mr. Harry Witcombe who for many years served the community of Canvey, particularly C.I.S.C House.

Frances and Roland Prout

The Prout brothers represented Britain in the 1952 Olympic Games as canoeists. In 1981 with eight others they represented Britain in the World Canoeing Championships in Macon France for 4 days. Frances and Roland had previously raced in Paris in an international regatta 2 years earlier.

Matt Simpson

Matt Simpson was born on Canvey 24yrs ago, he attended William Read School and Furtherwick Park School. Matt trained and played football for Island Boys while at school, he also played rugby for The Essex Schools team. Whilst at Furtherwick Park he became champion Shot Putter at all age groups, he won the English title three times, he was third in the European juniors, second in the American Universities Championship, second in The World Student Games, He got a Gold at the Commonwealth Games 1994 at Toronto, Canda. Matt Simpson is studying at Florida University, America.

Wendy Hale

Wendy Hale plays netball for England in the Senior Squad Netball Team. When she was at Furtherwick Park School she represented England in the under 16's, and when at SEEVIC Benfleet the under 18's, and then under 21 's level, in the Home Internation which she Captained for a tour of the West Indies.

In 1985 and 1990 she toured Australia in the Senior Squad. In the Home Internationals she has toured Trinidad, Jamaica and Australia. Wendy is a bank clerk at the National Westminster Bank, she plays local netball for the New Cambell Club, Dagenham, and Barn Hall Wickford.

Rob Denmark

Robert Denmark is 25 years old, he attended Leigh Beck school, and Furtherwick Park School, from there he went on to Newcastle University for three years where he obtained a B.A. (Honours) specialising in sport. Rob was for two years a Play Leader at Kings George's Playing Fields summer camp, which school children attended during the school holiday.

In 1992 he reached the Olympic finals in Barcelona and came 7th. In 1993 he was champion of the Europa Cup. He became a top class runner in 1994 when he won silver medal at the Commonwealth Games in Victoria, Toronto Canada. This year Rob has been presented with "The Professional Award" from the management and Sports Staff of BBC Essex. The Chairman of Basildon Council, Councillor Frank Tomlin has presented Rob with a cut glass decanter and a Gold Bascard, which entitles him to use all Basildon training facilities free. This Gold Bascard is only awarded to outstanding local athletes.

Wayne Barsby

Son of Geoff Barsby in District News. 1992/93/94 National Karate Grand Chapion. Wayne is holder of nine national titles. Also a member of E.K.A British Squad.

Dr Feelgood

My brother Christopher White started his acting career by playing the Artful Dodger in "Oliver" at The Palace Theatre when he was 13 years old, he was also in Westside Story under the direction of the late Alexander Bridge, he attended Leigh Beck School and Furtherwick Park School, he then went on to do 2 years at Aid Foster Stage School and two years at Phildene Drama School, he appeared in "Dixon of Dock Green" Paul Temple, Bachelor Father, Doctor in Charge, The Village, Please Sir, he was also in the Danny La Rue film "Our Miss Fred". His stage name was Christopher Fenwick.

Chris was the Manager of Dr. Feelgood Rock and Roll Band. All the members of the original band lived on Canvey they started off as a Jug Band when they were school children busking outside the various Pubs playing a gig whenever anybody would let them, in the middle of a Bingo session, even in the middle of a Keep Fit Demostation at the Casino Ballroom or a Canvey Carnival event. One time when still a Jug Band they won the talent contest at King's Holiday Camp, and managed to be allowed to play at the Oysterfleet by twisting Mr. Mick Saunders arm who was the Proprietor, it is coincidental that when Lee Brilleaux became ill and they had to stop touring they ran the Club as Dr. Feelgood's Music Bar, giving young musicians a chance a play. The club has now been demolished as plans had already been passed for a New Hotel, which it is hoped will be finished the middle of June 1995, Chris Fenwick has been asked to be the new Manager, as half his life his has been spent in Hotel's around the world he hopes to make it a success.

When the Feelgood's played around the local jaunts, they even ventured over to Kent to get a broader horizon, complete with their equipment in an old pram they bought at a Jumble Sale, little did they know then that they were to play all over the world. They formed Dr. Feelgood after playing Southend haunts, playing a gig in Holland, which Chris, who was then 18 years was in Holland, when he met someone who was interested in hiring British bands, seizing his chance, Chris said he had a band in England, He came home and told the Feelgood's he'd fixed them a tour. If he bought a van could he manage them. Whilst Chris was still at drama school Lee who had just left Newcastle University, who in 1964 had been in a pop group with The Big Figure called The Roamers. They played Canvey Weddings and Working Men's clubs. But Wilko used to make more money busking with his brother Malcolm on comb and paper. It was around this time that Lee had seen them in the street and got ideas of his own. For five years Wilko put his guitar away, he decided his was going to be a poet.

The Figure was playing in pop groups up and down the country. The others into jug bands Ginger beer jar, hubble bubble and shears were among the implements used in "Chrissy White's Jug Band, though Chris himself was a Musician".

John Sparkes appeared on twelve string hence his chord style of bass playing. Lee played banjo and did the vocals. When the jug band broke Lee joined a blues band called The Fix. Then he and Sparko were both in the Pigboy Charlie band. Dr. Feelgood was formed with Chris as their Manager in 1972 after two successful tours of Holland and backing Heinz at the Southend Rock Festival and the Wembly Rock Festival, early 1974 they broke into the London Pub circuit. They made an immediate impact on the press, the punters and the business. Paul Conroy and Nigel Kerr signed them to the Charisma Agency, and Andrew Lauder signed them to United Artists, the record contract enabled them to relinquish their day jobs and to accept gigs beyond day tripping.

In 1974 they toured nationally with Bringley Sdwarz and Dave Edmonds billed as the "New Favourites tour" acknowledging their influences they recorded their first album "Down by the Jetty" in mono, in February 1975 they participated in the notorious Naughty Rhythms Tour and emerged national stars, later that year completed their first tour as headliners, promoting their second album "Malpractice. After a debut at the annual convention in San Diego, they embarked on their first United States tour. Back in England their third album "Stupidity" recorded live in Sheffield and Southend reach -ed No.1 and remained in the top 50 for 2 months, they were then regarded as one of the most exciting acts in Britain, there followed another top 10 album Sneaking Suspicion.

In March 1977, John Mayo from Harlow replaced the manic guitarist Wilko Johnson, an audition for this replacement was held at Feelgood House, in Central Wall Road, if you happened to be driving through Benfleet that day you would have thought that Canvey had been invaded as every train from London seem to carry hundreds of youths carrying guitars.

September 1977 the modified line up made its final debut with Nick Lowe producing "Be Seeing You" from which came the hit single "She's a wind up", after more American and Continental touring, they recorded their sixth album "Private Practice".

The band was always well known as being down to earth and friendly, spent the next 10 years or so travelling the world, which 18,000 people attended the shows.

Lee in particular threw himself into the performance with energy and gusto, shaking his head like a madman, showering torrents of sweat everywhere, singing songs like "Milk and Alcohol and old favourites like "See you later Alligator" which went gold in Sweden.

Gypie quit the band in 1981 to be replaced by Johnney Guitar and in 1981 Sparko and the Figure left to spend more time with their families. Phil Mitchell, Kevin Morris and Gorden Russell formed the new formation of the group, finally Steve Walwyn and Dave Bronze taking over on guitar and bass only front man Lee remained, as always dressed in a suit, strutting round the stage, snapping back and forth as he growled out the lyrics. Lee was a charismatic focal always for every Feelgood show, always the showman always polite. Always a true gent, sadly Lee was diagnosed in 1993 as having Lymphoma, a form of cancer, while in remission from the illness Lee made two final concert appearances at Dr. Feelgood Music Bar. In April 1994 Lee lost his year long battle against the illness. The singer was one of the giants of the local music scene over the last quarter of the century, but a very modest and unassuming man.

A special tribute concert was held on May 10th which would have been Lee's 42 birthday, at his music bar, this was attended by fans all over the Country and Europe.

THRILL: Steve Walwyn and Lee Brilleaux on stage in Paris

left to right: Gordon Russell, Phil Mitchell, Kevin Morris, manager Chris Fenwick and Lee Brilleaux.

Conclusion

Canvey Island today has almost reached its peak for development as an Industrial, urban and holiday community.

This small area of five miles in width and two miles long can barely offer today, more than a few acres of its marshland for future development.

The Island is noted for independence and unity of its peoples. This has been a necessity, for the past development in the last thirty years and has leant the co-operation of much local interest, and the individual members of the community have directly been involved. This has been due to the fact that from an early age the land was divided into small areas as the former plan of Canvey's enterprising Mr. Hester.

The post war developers were the grand children whose former parents had bought their plots by easy payments to erect a little bungalow, or to pitch their tent in order to take the fresh air of the Thames.

For the existing development to take place on Canvey Island, many plots of land were communed together for industrial sites.

The contracting arrangements that were necessary for this complex involvement has held an added common interest for a vast majority of the people and even today many toasts still can be heard for dear Mr. Hester in the old Lobster Smack Inn.

I have tried to show the gradual development of the Island, not just by pure fact, but by contributing some personal and long lived accounts which I think show the proudness and indepence of the people and see, to have been a prominent factor in determining the Island growth and prosperity.

In 1974 Canvey and Benfleet became united, becoming Castle Point District Council, a few years ago Mr. Terry Holding presented to the council a chain of office and regalia when they became Castle Point Borough Council.

9781780350981

ND - #0109 - 060826 - C0 - 210/148/10 - PB - 9781780350981 - Gloss Lamination